The Adversary System

A Description and Defense

The Adversary System
A Description and Defense

Stephan Landsman

American Enterprise Institute for Public Policy Research
Washington and London

Stephan Landsman is professor of law at the Cleveland-Marshall College of Law.

Library of Congress Cataloging in Publication Data
Landsman, Stephan.
    The adversary system.

    (AEI studies ; 390)
    1. Adversary system (Law)—United States.
I. Title. II. Series.
KF384.L26   1983   347.73   83-15486
ISBN 0-8447-3533-7   347.307

AEI Studies 390

© 1984 by American Enterprise Institute for Public Policy Research, Washington, D.C., and London. All rights reserved. No part of this publication may be used or reproduced in any manner whatsoever without permission in writing from the American Enterprise Institute except in the case of brief quotations embodied in news articles, critical articles, or reviews. The views expressed in the publications of the American Enterprise Institute are those of the authors and do not necessarily reflect the views of the staff, advisory panels, officers, or trustees of AEI.

"American Enterprise Institute" and ⟨AEI⟩ are registered service marks of the American Enterprise Institute for Public Policy Research.

Printed in the United States of America

Contents

	FOREWORD	
1	THE ADVERSARY SYSTEM DEFINED	1
	Neutral and Passive Fact Finder 2	
	Party Presentation of Evidence 4	
	Highly Structured Forensic Procedure 4	
2	THE HISTORY OF THE ADVERSARY SYSTEM	
	Medieval Procedure 8	
	The Rise of the Jury 10	
	Development of Preadversarial Legal Institutions between 1200 and 1700 14	
	The Establishment of the Adversary System 18	
3	NONADVERSARIAL ELEMENTS IN THE AMERICAN JUDICIAL SYSTEM	26
	The Criminal Process 26	
	Nonadversarial Reforms 28	
4	CRITICISMS OF THE ADVERSARY SYSTEM CONSIDERED	34
	The Pace of Adjudication 34	
	The Discovery of Material Truth 36	
	Access to the Judicial System 39	
	The Power of the Attorney 41	
	Conflicting Judicial Responsibilities 41	
5	DEFENSE OF THE ADVERSARY SYSTEM	44
	Benefits of Party Control of Litigation 44	
	Constitutional Recognition of Adversarial Procedures 47	
	Comparison of Adversarial and Inquisitorial Processes 48	
6	USING NONADVERSARIAL MEANS TO RESOLVE DISPUTES	52
	SELECTED BIBLIOGRAPHY	

The American Enterprise Institute for Public Policy Research, established in 1943, is a nonpartisan research and educational organization supported by foundations, corporations, and the public at large. Its purpose is to assist policy makers, scholars, businessmen, the press, and the public by providing objective analysis of national and international issues. Views expressed in the institute's publications are those of the authors and do not necessarily reflect the views of the staff, advisory panels, officers, or trustees of AEI.

Council of Academic Advisers

Paul W. McCracken, *Chairman, Edmund Ezra Day University Professor of Business Administration, University of Michigan*
*Kenneth W. Dam, *Harold J. and Marion F. Green Professor of Law, University of Chicago*
Donald C. Hellmann, *Professor of Political Science and International Studies, University of Washington*
D. Gale Johnson, *Eliakim Hastings Moore Distinguished Service Professor of Economics and Chairman, Department of Economics, University of Chicago*
Robert A. Nisbet, *Adjunct Scholar, American Enterprise Institute*
Herbert Stein, *A. Willis Robertson Professor of Economics, University of Virginia*
James Q. Wilson, *Henry Lee Shattuck Professor of Government, Harvard University*
*On leave for government service.

Executive Committee

Richard B. Madden, *Chairman of the Board*
William J. Baroody, Jr., *President*
James G. Affleck

Willard C. Butcher
Paul F. Oreffice
Richard D. Wood

Tait Trussell,
   Vice President, Administration
Joseph J. Brady,
   Vice President, Development

Edward Styles, *Director of Publications*

Program Directors

Russell Chapin, *Legislative Analyses*
Denis P. Doyle, *Education Policy Studies*
Marvin Esch, *Seminars and Programs*
Thomas F. Johnson, *Economic Policy Studies*
Marvin H. Kosters,
   Government Regulation Studies
Jack A. Meyer, *Health Policy Studies*
Howard R. Penniman/Austin Ranney,
   Political and Social Processes
Robert J. Pranger, *International Programs*

Periodicals

AEI Economist, Herbert Stein,
   Editor
Public Opinion, Seymour Martin
   Lipset and Ben J. Wattenberg,
   Co-Editors; Everett Carll Ladd,
   Senior Editor; Karlyn H. Keene,
   Managing Editor
Regulation, Anne Brunsdale,
   Managing Editor

Foreword

The mission of the American Enterprise Institute is to promote a continuing dialogue and probing debate over the important public policy issues that confront the nation and the states. To develop a better understanding of our institutional arrangements, of the fundamental assumptions on which our government and society are based, and of the systems and procedures that we employ is vital to a proper resolution of public policy issues.

Surprisingly little has been written on the adversary system, perhaps because nearly everyone takes it for granted. In a day when major new compensation systems are being proposed, this book, *The Adversary System: A Description and a Defense,* seeks to fill a long-felt need for a better understanding of the basic features of the adversary system. This study will stimulate a renewed examination of the fundamental principles of the adversary system and how it protects our rights and serves society.

WILLIAM J. BAROODY, JR.
President
American Enterprise Institute

1
The Adversary System Defined

> *The philosophy of adjudication that is expressed in "the adversary system" is, speaking generally, a philosophy that insists on keeping distinct the function of the advocate, on the one hand, from that of the judge, or of the judge from that of jury, on the other. The decision of the case is for the judge, or for the judge and jury. That decision must be as objective and as free from bias as it possibly can. The Constitution of Massachusetts provides—in language that in its idiom calls at once to mind the spirit of a great age, the Age of the Enlightenment and of the American and French Revolutions—that "It is the right of every citizen to be tried by judges as free, impartial and independent as the lot of humanity will admit." If the judge is to perform that high function—a function which the Constitution recognizes may put human nature to a severe test—then the rules of procedure that govern a trial must be such that they do not compel or invite him to depart from the difficult role in which he is cast. It is not his place to take sides. He must withhold judgment until all the evidence has been examined and all the arguments have been heard.*[1]

Since at least the time of the American Revolution, courts in the United States have employed a system of procedure that depends upon a neutral and passive fact finder (either judge or jury) to resolve disputes on the basis of information provided by contending parties during formal proceedings. This sort of dispute-resolving mechanism is most frequently referred to as the adversary system. Whether to continue relying upon the adversary system has become a subject of intense debate in the United States. Among the critics of the adversary system are some of the most powerful members of the legal establishment, including the chief justice of the United States Supreme Court and the American Bar Association Commission on Evaluation of Professional Standards. Chief Justice Burger has suggested that the adversary system as presently constituted denies justice to litigants, impairs faith in the courts, and raises the specter of the "breakdown" of the judicial machinery. He has suggested substantial modification of the system as a means of dealing with these problems. The American Bar Association Commission shares Justice Burger's concerns. In its Model Rules of Professional Conduct, first presented in January 1980, it proposes revisions of the lawyer's code of ethics designed to reduce substantially the adversarial nature of attorney behavior. In light of such attacks, this seems an appropriate time to reexamine the implications and the value of the adversary system.

The first step in assessing the worth of the adversary system is to define what we mean when we use the term. The adversary process should not be viewed as a single technique or collection of techniques; it is a unified concept that works by use of a number of interconnecting procedures, each of real importance to the process as a whole. The central precept of the adversary process is that out of the sharp clash of proofs presented by adversaries in a highly structured forensic setting is most likely to come the information upon which a neutral and passive decision maker can base the resolution of a litigated dispute acceptable to both the parties and society. This formulation is advantageous not only because it expresses the overarching adversarial concept, but also because it identifies the method to be utilized in adjudication (the sharp clash of proofs in a highly structured setting), the actors essential to the process (two adversaries and a decision maker), the nature of their functions (presentation of proofs and adjudication of disputes, respectively), and the goal of the entire endeavor (the resolution of disputes in a manner acceptable to the parties and to society).

Like any brief definition of a complex subject the foregoing description of the adversary system fails to indicate some of the most important principles and practices inherent in adversary methodology. The key elements in the system—utilization of a neutral and passive fact finder, reliance on party presentation of evidence, and use of a highly structured forensic procedure—must be more fully discussed to present an accurate picture. This additional information will also be of particular importance in helping to assess the value and shortcomings of the adversary process.

Neutral and Passive Fact Finder

The adversary system relies on a neutral and passive decision maker to adjudicate disputes after they have been aired by the adversaries in a contested proceeding. He is expected to refrain from making any judgments until the conclusion of the contest and is prohibited from becoming actively involved in the gathering of evidence or the settlement of the case. Adversary theory suggests that if the decision maker strays from the passive role, he runs a serious risk of prematurely committing himself to one or another version of the facts and of failing to appreciate the value of all the evidence.

Adversary theory further suggests that neutrality and passivity are essential not only to ensure an evenhanded consideration of each case, but also to convince society at large that the judicial system is trustworthy. When a decision maker becomes an active questioner or otherwise participates in a case, he is likely to be perceived as partisan rather than neutral. Judicial passivity helps to ensure the appearance of fairness.

One of the most significant implications of the adoption of the principles of neutrality and passivity is that they tend to commit the adversary system to the objective of resolving disputes rather than searching for material truth. The judicial process is generally used to satisfy two objectives: first, the search for truth, and second, the resolution of disputes between contending parties. Although most court systems seek to accomplish both these goals, the procedural mechanisms best suited to the achievement of each are different. Where judges are assigned an active, inquisitorial part in the litigation process, they will be expected to undertake an uninhibited search for truth. Perhaps the best examples of this approach are to be found in the justice systems of the Socialist states of Eastern Europe. Where judges are assigned a neutral and passive function, however, they will, in all likelihood, be expected to devote their energies to resolving the disputes framed by the litigants. The American adversary system has traditionally accepted the latter approach and thereby favored the goal of resolving disputes.

The second major implication of insistence on the neutrality and passivity of the decision maker is that it favors the use of lay juries rather than professional judges. Judges are deeply involved in the management of the lawsuits. They are constantly being called upon to make rulings and otherwise direct the contest. Their passivity and neutrality are likely to be strained as they perform these functions. Except in cases of unusual notoriety, juries are unlikely to face similar strains or to become embroiled in the contest. Further, the members of the jury are likely to be free of those predispositions judges develop because of their training and daily experience in the handling of legal matters. In addition, because the jury comprises a number of individuals, the prejudices of a single juror are not likely to destroy the capacity of the group to render a fair decision. This must be contrasted with the situation of the solitary judge whose biases can easily influence the decisions he renders. Finally, potential jurors can be questioned before they are permitted to take a seat on the jury and can be excluded if biased. There is no similar mechanism to ensure judicial neutrality. For all these reasons the jury is more likely than the judge to meet adversarial expectations of neutrality and passivity and is therefore favored in adversarial proceedings.

Party Presentation of Evidence

Intimately connected with the requirements of decision maker passivity and neutrality is the procedural principle that the parties are responsible for producing all the evidence upon which the decision will be based. This principle insulates the fact finder from involvement in the contest. It also encourages the adversaries to find and present their most persuasive evidence. Adherence to this principle affords the decision maker the advantage of seeing what each litigant believes to be his most consequential proof. It also focuses the litigation upon the questions of greatest importance to the parties, making more likely a decision tailored to their needs. The benefits of such an approach may be measured in economic terms. A judge-dominated procedure increases the likelihood that the needs of the litigants will not be fully appreciated or satisfied. When this is the case "impositional costs" (those caused by an unbargained for and poorly tailored solution) are substantially increased. Such costs can, in large measure, be avoided in a system relying on participant direction and control.

Because of the potential complexity of legal questions and the intricacy of the legal mechanism, parties generally cannot manage their own lawsuits. Rather, they, and the adversary system, have come to rely upon a class of skilled professional advocates to assemble and to present the testimony upon which decisions will be based. The advocates are expected to provide the forensic talents necessary to organize the evidence and to formulate the legal issues. If the lawyers fail to carry out their duty, development of the case will be impeded, and the adversary process may be undermined. Failure of counsel may also draw the judge into the contest either in search of material truth or in an attempt to ensure a balanced presentation. In either situation, judicial intervention can interfere with the neutral evaluation of the case.

Highly Structured Forensic Procedure

Elaborate sets of rules to govern the pretrial and posttrial periods (rules of procedure), the trial itself (rules of evidence), and the behavior of counsel (rules of ethics) are all important to the adversary system. Rules of procedure serve at least two functions in the adversary scheme. First, they structure litigation to produce a climactic confrontation between the parties in a single trial session or set of trial sessions. Such a confrontation yields the evidence upon which the decision will be based and diminishes the opportunity for the fact finder to undertake a potentially biasing independent investigation. Second, adversarial rules of procedure help to ensure the fairness of the contest by affording each litigant an equal opportunity to make the best possible case. The primary mechanism for ensuring equality is pretrial discovery, a technique allowing each party to examine his opponent's proof.

The trial or evidence rules protect the integrity of the testimonial segment of adversary proceedings. They prohibit the use of evidence that is likely to be unreliable and thereby insulate the trier from misleading information. The evidence rules also prohibit the use of evidence that poses a serious threat of exciting unfair prejudice against one of the parties. Rather than allow the use of such information the adversary system seeks to preserve the neutrality and passivity of the decision maker by a strictly enforced prohibition. Rules of evidence also enhance the power of the attorney to control the presentation of facts by providing him with a precisely formulated set of principles to measure the admissibility of every piece of evidence. In this way the rules confine the authority of the judge in managing the proceedings. Judges are not free to pick and choose the evidence they think most appropriate; rather, they are bound to obey the previously fixed evidentiary prescripts.

Since the rough-and-tumble of adversary procedure exacerbates the natural tendency of advocates to seek to win by any means available, the adversary system employs rules of ethics to control the behavior of counsel. To ensure the integrity of the process certain tactics are forbidden, including those designed to harass or to intimidate an opponent as well as those intended to mislead or to prejudice the trier of fact. In addition to their prohibitory function, the rules of ethics are designed to promote vigorous adversarial contests by requiring that each attorney zealously represent his client's interests at all times. To ensure zeal, attorneys are required to give their undivided loyalty to their clients.

Reliance on elaborate sets of rules to structure the adversary process led to the establishment of courts of appeals. These courts see to it that litigants and judges comply with mandated rules and procedures. Appellate judges review the records of trial proceedings and determine whether the various legal prescriptions have been obeyed. If error is found, the appellate courts are free to use any one of a number of remedies to redress the harm done. Appellate review also encourages attorneys and judges at the trial level to adhere to the requirements of the law in order to avoid reversal on appeal.

The following chapters of this study explore both the history and the value of the adversary system. Chapter 2 examines certain facets of English and American legal history in an effort to identify the reasons for the development of the adversary approach. Chapter 3 assesses the condition of the adversary system in the United States today, focusing especially on aspects of adversary procedure that have been altered or are under attack. Chapter 4 addresses the criticisms leveled against the adversary system and attempts to refute those criticisms. Chapter 5 presents a defense of the adversary system. The advantages of the system are detailed and the primary procedural alternative to the adversary method, the inquisitorial process, is analyzed. Finally, Chapter 6 briefly considers situations in which adversary procedure need not be employed.

Notes

1. Lon L. Fuller, "The Adversary System," in Harold Berman, ed., *Talks on American Law* (New York: Random House, 1961), pp. 34–35.

2
The History of the Adversary System

An examination of the history of the adversary system provides a variety of insights about the values it vindicates and the reasons for its present structure. Although the adversary system as a whole did not begin to coalesce until the 1700s, its components had been developing for centuries. What made the system come together when it did is not easy to say. Its synthesis is, however, clearly associated with the social and economic changes that occurred between 1700 and 1800. These changes included the rise of the modern industrial state, the acceptance of a thoroughgoing doctrine of individual liberty, and the demise of the static social tranquility that had marked both England and America in the preceding epoch. From all this, one can glean some idea of the values served by the adversary system. These values include freedom from restraint on economic and political action, tolerance of change in both business and social relations, and willingness to adjudicate questions not previously considered by society.

Despite the great changes reflected in the rise of the adversary system, Anglo-American legal history reveals the remarkable inclination of both English and American society to preserve existing judicial institutions. Rather than fabricate new procedures, jurists and lawyers in the English-speaking world repeatedly adapted existing processes to new needs. This is strikingly apparent in the case of the development of the jury. Between 1300 and 1800 the jury was transformed from an instrument of royal inquiry to a neutral and passive fact finder inclined to protect individuals from government overreaching. This significant change in objective was accomplished while jury procedure retained much of its original structure.

The tendency to preserve the existing legal machinery may have insulated British and American society from the worst excesses of government tyranny. Again, experience with the jury provides a good example. The existence of jury procedure in the thirteenth century blocked the introduction of inquisitorial methods into England. By adhering to existing legal methods, England avoided the adoption of the rack as a means of seeking justice. Unwillingness to change has not always been advantageous for English and American courts. It led to excessive tolerance of delay and technicality. Still, the historical lesson about the value of preserving traditional legal methods should not be overlooked.

Medieval Procedure

The adversary method of resolving disputes did not appear, fully formed, at a precise moment in history. Rather, it is one of the products of the slow evolution of English and American judicial procedure. To understand how the adversary system arose, one must go back at least to the eleventh century and examine the ancient precursors of present-day judicial practice.

The forensic clash of the parties in the adversary system seems so like combat, it is tempting to suggest that the real source of the adversary process was the ancient mode of resolving disputes referred to as trial by battle. Historical evidence does not, however, support this proposition.

Trial by battle was a means of settling conflicts that required the disputants or their champions to engage in physical combat until one side or the other yielded (by speaking the word "craven"), was decisively defeated or, in certain serious criminal matters, was slain. Judicial officers oversaw the battle, which commenced after each of the combatants had taken a solemn oath that his cause was just, had invoked the judgment of God, and had declared that he had made no use of sorcery or enchantment.

Trial by battle was in common use throughout most of northern Europe in the early Middle Ages. It was not employed in England, however, until after the Norman Conquest in 1066. The fact of its late introduction into Britain, its Norman sponsorship, its potentially drastic consequences, and its bias in favor of the rich, who either had martial skills or could hire those with such skills, have led most commentators to surmise that it was never a popular or influential form of adjudication in England.

Battle was generally the last resort of the medieval English courts, and there were several alternatives to it. The two most important alternative means of resolving disputes were wager of law and ordeal. In wager of law, one of the litigants swore a precisely prescribed oath that his claims were true. He was then obliged to produce a certain number of other persons, usually referred to as compurgators, who were to support his oath by means of oaths of their own. If all was performed in the proper way, the oath taker won his case. Historian Theodore Plucknett described the wager of law as a "character test" in which the oath taker established his case by demonstrating his good standing in the community.[1]

The ordeal was a form of adjudication popular throughout medieval Europe. It was premised upon the idea that God would intervene and by miraculous sign indicate which litigant was in the right. A priest usually administered an oath before the ordeal, and, quite frequently, the ordeal was conducted on church grounds. Plucknett indicates that in England the primary forms of ordeal called for the litigant to carry a red-hot iron bar, to place an arm in boiling water, or to be immersed in deep water. In the first two instances, if the litigant's burns did not fester after a prescribed period, he was held to be in the right. In the latter case, the litigant was declared innocent if he briefly sank rather than floated.

In most cases more than one form of trial might be applicable. A crucial function of the medieval court was to decide which method to employ. This was usually done after the plaintiff had orally stated his claim to the court and had supported it with various proofs, sometimes logically persuasive evidence, more often oaths from individuals not directly involved in the litigation. The defendant was limited to a single defense, denial of the plaintiff's claim. Based upon these preliminary proceedings the court would enter a "medial judgment" fixing the form of trial and designating the party required to make the proof. Being permitted to make the proof was generally considered an advantage because the maker (especially in cases of wager of law and ordeal) was likely to succeed. The outcome of the wager, ordeal, or battle was the exclusive basis upon which the dispute was resolved, and no other evidence would be considered on the ultimate issue of the case.

All the medieval methods of trial were premised upon divine intervention. Direct heavenly intercession was postulated with respect to ordeal and battle, while eternal damnation was supposed to enforce the oath-taking mechanism. Emphasis was clearly on the judgment of God rather than that of man (though the medial judgment procedure suggests some tempering of this idea). As befitted such a system, there was very little use of evidence. The process was not orally contentious. There was no need for any sort of fact finding because no facts were to be deduced from evidence. Activity in the courts was, to an overwhelming degree, carried on by the parties rather than by advocates, and advocates could do only a limited amount. Because the court relied on divine revelation, there was no appellate process.

Although none of the medieval methods was even remotely adversarial, medieval forms of procedure did contribute to the formulation of adversarial concepts in at least two ways. First, they helped to establish the principle that the parties to a dispute are to play the preeminent part in the procedure leading to its resolution. This idea of active party participation is fundamental to the adversary system and is continuously present in English law from the medieval period onwards. Second, at the same time that medieval practice ceded a large role to the parties, it circumscribed the part to be played by judicial officials. Although judges would eventually gain a far more important role in resolving disputes, the early restraints on judicial activity at least helped to establish a tradition that restricts judicial control of litigation.

By the middle of the thirteenth century all the medieval procedures had been either banned or seriously criticized. In 1215 the Fourth Lateran Council prohibited church participation in trial by ordeal. This prohibition effectively ended the practice because participation by priests had been a fundamental component of the process. At about the same time, canon and lay critics began a sustained attack on wager of law and trial by battle. The decline of the medieval methods led to the development of new judicial practices between the thirteenth and seventeenth centuries. These practices formed the foundation upon which the adversary system was erected in the eighteenth and nineteenth centuries.

The Rise of the Jury

Without doubt the most important new practice was the use of the jury to resolve disputes in English courts. The origins of the jury have not been authoritatively established. Some historians propound a continental genesis (Plucknett, for example, points to France during the reign of Louis the Pious, circa 829 A.D.), while others advocate an early Anglo-Saxon beginning.[2] However it originally arose, by the end of the twelfth century the jury had been incorporated into the English judicial process. Its acceptance at that time can be linked to the decline of the medieval forms of procedure. As ordeal, battle, and wager shrank in significance, trial by jury expanded to replace them.

Sir William Holdsworth and Theodore Plucknett suggest that criminal and civil jury practice evolved along separate though related lines during the formative period from the end of the twelfth century to the middle of the fifteenth century.[3] The first kind of criminal jury to appear was the jury of presentment, or grand jury. This jury consisted of a group of prominent citizens called together at royal insistence to report on the misdeeds of local citizens and to prepare indictments for the prosecution of accused malefactors. In the early days, indicted defendants were tried either by ordeal or by wager of law. (Battle could only be used in privately initiated criminal cases.) As ordeal and wager fell into disuse, the judiciary naturally gravitated toward the use of a second jury (often containing several members of the original presentment jury) to decide the question of guilt or innocence. (In the case of privately pursued criminal actions, the defendant, as early as the twelfth century, could purchase from the king the opportunity to be tried by a jury rather than to engage in battle.) Although criminal jury procedure was quite variable during the thirteenth and fourteenth centuries, the size of the trial jury eventually came to be fixed at twelve men. From the earliest times the jurors had to be drawn from the neighborhood in which the crime had taken place.

On the civil side, Henry II, in the late part of the twelfth century, introduced the assize as a means of settling certain disputes concerning the ownership of land. As had been the case with the criminal jury, the assize was composed of a group of prominent citizens from the community in which the dispute arose. Members of the assize were selected by the king's officers and were charged with the responsibility of deciding disputes upon the basis of their personal knowledge. Gradually, such groups came to be used to resolve conflicts other than those concerning the ownership of land. The popularity of this form of adjudication led to its ever expanding use, and it eventually became the procedure of choice for virtually every civil cause of action.

The early juries were not the neutral and passive fact-finding mechanism they eventually became when incorporated within the adversary system. At first, the jury was little more than another sort of formal and inscrutable trial, like ordeal or wager of law. In its early days the jury heard no evidence and rendered its decision on no rational basis. Apparently, divine guidance was relied upon to produce the proper result. Yet, even in its earliest avatars, the jury was an improvement over the medieval methods of proof. Jurors were selected from the locality in which the dispute arose and almost always included among their number some persons with knowledge of the events that were the focus of the litigation. As the jury mechanism matured, jurors were allowed as much as two weeks notice before jury trials. During the period between notice and trial, jurors were allowed to certify themselves of the facts in dispute by talking to the litigants and making private inquiries in the community. All of this tended to ensure that jurors would be, to some degree, informed of the facts in issue and therefore likely to make a reasoned decision.

The use of jurors from the neighborhood and reliance upon each juror's personal knowledge marked early jury procedure as inquisitorial rather than adversarial. The jury did not act as a neutral and passive fact finder, but as an active and inquiring body searching for material truth. The inquisitorial elements in jury procedure were long-lived in both England and the United States. To this day the grand jury functions as an inquisitorial body seeking evidence upon which to premise criminal indictments. As late as 1670 the English courts held in *Bushell's Case*[4] that jurors were free to reject the evidence presented in court and base their decision on private knowledge. (It has been argued that this aspect of the ruling in *Bushell's Case* is significantly anachronistic.) It was not until 1705 in civil cases and 1826 in criminal cases that jurors could be drawn from places other than the immediate locality in which the dispute arose (even if a change of venue were warranted because of local prejudice).

Although the jury was not by its nature adversarial, certain of its procedures and much of its early development paved the way for the growth of the adversary process. From 1300 to 1500 the jury developed many of the characteristics that would result in its becoming a neutral and passive adjudicator. By the middle of the 1300s, prospective jurors could be challenged by the parties and potentially biased jurors removed from the panel. Toward the end of the 1300s or in the early 1400s, contacts between litigants and jurors during the pendency of a case were significantly curtailed, thereby reducing the possibility of prejudice. By 1470 Fortesque in his famous volume, *In Praise of the Laws of England,* was able to describe jurors as impartial men who came to court with open minds.[5]

As already noted, jurors could, perhaps as late as 1670, rely upon their private knowledge in reaching a decision. From at least the fifteenth century on, however, jurors began to rely upon what was presented in court as the basis for their decision. Sources of in-court information included the arguments of counsel (often treated as the equivalent of testimony given under oath) and the testimony of witnesses. The use of a considerable volume of evidence had the effect of subtly shifting the function of the jury from active inquiry to passive review and analysis.

The juries assembled by the king's representatives in the twelfth and thirteenth centuries were quite clearly under the control of the government. They were specially selected by royal officials for the purpose of answering questions propounded on behalf of the king. Eventually, however, the jury became an independent entity unconnected with the objectives of the government. This change was undoubtedly facilitated by the increasingly neutral and passive functioning of the jury. Arguably, the jury had become by 1670, an independent agency capable of resisting government direction or control. Fundamental to the realization of this independence was the previously mentioned ruling in *Bushell's Case*. There, Chief Justice Vaughan flatly rejected the idea that the judiciary could control juries by the imposition of sanctions, thereby freeing the jury. (Plucknett suggests that evidence of the political independence of the jury may be found as early as 1544 when a jury refused to convict Throckmorton despite clear evidence of his involvement in Wyatt's rebellion.[6])

The growing neutrality, passivity, and independence of the jury had the effect of loosening the government's political hold on the judiciary. The presence of an independent jury relieved the judges of responsibility for unpopular or politically inexpedient decisions. The jury thereby insulated judges from political criticism and allowed them to develop a more evenhanded approach toward the litigants. The presence of an independent fact finder encouraged judges to concentrate their energies on questions of law. This specialization of function reduced the likelihood that judges would become embroiled in the search for evidence or the prosecution of the case.

The rise of the jury not only laid the groundwork for adversary procedure, it also inhibited the development of the inquisitorial process in England. In England the vacuum created by the Fourth Lateran Council's ban in 1215 of church participation in ordeals (and the related criticism of wager of law and battle) was filled by jury trial. On the continent a very different form of procedure was adopted, most frequently referred to as the Roman-canon system. It was the product of the combination of certain aspects of ancient Roman law with judicial principles developed in European ecclesiastical circles. By the thirteenth century this amalgamation of the Roman and canon approaches had replaced the ordeal and other forms of medieval adjudication throughout much of Europe.

The Roman-canon system placed fundamental emphasis on active inquiry by the judge to uncover truth. He was charged with the duty of investigating the case, gathering the proof, and rendering the decision. He was obviously the central figure in the litigation, and his actions determined the outcome. The scope of the judge's powers was so extensive (and such a radical departure from the ordeal, which purported to rely on the judgment of God) that it was thought prudent in the criminal context to limit his authority by means of strict evidentiary requirements for the establishment of guilt. The judge could not find a defendant guilty unless two eyewitnesses were produced who had observed the gravamen of the crime. If two such witnesses were not available, conviction could only be obtained if the defendant confessed. Circumstantial evidence was never sufficient, in itself, to warrant conviction. The effect of these evidentiary rules was to make it impossible to obtain convictions in many cases unless the defendant was willing to confess. To extract the necessary confessions, Roman-canon process authorized the use of torture. Torture became a tool of judicial inquiry and was used to generate the evidence upon which the defendant would be condemned.

Rather than adopt the Roman-canon approach the English elected to rely upon the jury. By so doing Britain rejected the straitjacketing evidentiary rules of the ecclesiastical courts, the active and inquiring judicial officer, and the use of torture to obtain confessions. The jury made England resistant to Roman-canon ideas and thereby opened English courts at an early date to a broad spectrum of evidence to be assessed by an increasingly neutral and passive fact finder. The English chose to utilize an existing form of procedure to meet the needs of society. They thereby maintained traditional protections and avoided the adoption of a new and, in significant ways, oppressive alternative.

Development of Preadversarial Legal Institutions between 1200 and 1700

Between the thirteenth and seventeenth centuries a number of legal institutions besides the jury underwent changes that paved the way for adversarial procedure. Lawyers rose to prominence both as advocates and as judicial officers. In the early 1300s requirements were established concerning the education and conduct of those who would be allowed to argue cases in the king's courts. In time the advocates formed special organizations for the training and governance of the bar called the Inns of Court. The Inns produced lawyers highly skilled in court procedure and disputation. These men formed the nucleus of a legal profession that would eventually assert exclusive control over the judicial machinery.

As the jury's investigative role diminished, the advocates' trial responsibilities increased. Lawyers undertook the job of supplying the jury with evidence upon which decisions would be based. By 1600, lawyers had established their special status as masters of the evidentiary process. One recognition of this status was the adoption of the concept of attorney-client privilege around 1577. Lawyers were granted a special exemption from the obligation to provide evidence if it was originally provided to them by their clients. Although the privilege was first premised upon the dignity of the attorney, the rule clearly facilitated the lawyer's freewheeling search for evidence by insulating him from compulsion to disclose information obtained from his client. Seldom could anyone else claim such protection.

Lawyers came to dominate not only the advocacy process but the judiciary as well. By the thirteenth century, English law and procedure had become sufficiently technical to warrant the designation of full-time judges. At first, the judges were drawn from among the king's retainers. These men functioned as civil servants and traced their allegiance directly to the sovereign. But by the close of the thirteenth century the legal profession had wrested control of the judiciary away from civil servants. From 1300 on, judges would be appointed only from the ranks of serjeants, a small group that constituted the elite of the bar. This placed the judiciary firmly in the hands of lawyers and linked judicial concerns to advocate interests.

The professionalization of the judiciary led to ever more complex law and procedure. Technicality had the effect of isolating the judges and their work from the rest of the government. While this isolation was eventually to have negative consequences (a rigid preoccupation with form and excessive tolerance of delay), it did foster judicial independence. Reliance on a small group of elite judges also had the effect of inhibiting the establishment of any sizable judicial bureaucracy. Such a bureaucracy in several European countries had facilitated the adoption of methods dependent on extensive judicial inquiry rather than on party presentation. Its absence in England made inquisitorial methods impractical.

The transformation of the jury and the legal profession was accompanied by important changes in the English attitude toward witnesses and the value of their testimony. Through the fifteenth century the testimony of witnesses was not highly valued. Voluntary testimony was viewed with suspicion, and witnesses could not be compelled to testify against their will. In the sixteenth century the presentation of testimonial evidence grew dramatically. In accordance with the Marian statutes of 1554–1555, justices of the peace were charged with the duty of securing evidence and testimony in criminal proceedings. Professor John Langbein of the University of Chicago Law School has argued that the designation of the justice of the peace as an evidence-gathering prosecutorial officer was of crucial importance to the survival of jury procedure in criminal cases. He notes that, for unknown reasons, by the start of the sixteenth century juries had ceased to be self-informing. Without the justice of the peace to provide a steady flow of information to the jury, the usefulness of that body would be thoroughly undermined.[7] In the early 1560s the enactment of legislation allowing courts to compel witnesses to testify also helped to alter English attitudes toward witnesses. This legislation placed a stamp of approval on oral testimony as a source of information for the increasingly passive and uninformed jury. Both developments helped open the way to adversarial evidentiary procedure. They shifted attention from each juror's private knowledge toward witness testimony given in open court.

To facilitate the evaluation of testimonial and other evidence the English courts, after the enactment of the Marian statutes, accelerated their efforts to fashion rules of evidence. The judiciary developed rules prohibiting the use of certain sorts of misleading and untrustworthy material (for example, the testimony of proven perjurers). Other types of protective rules were advanced, including limitations upon the use of a wife's testimony against her husband. At the same time, previously established evidentiary rules were being refined, including the "best evidence" rule (limiting use of secondary sources to prove the contents of a writing), the opinion rule (controlling the use of opinion testimony), and the hearsay rule (barring the use of certain out-of-court statements). These rules did not prohibit the introduction of all misleading evidence, nor did they seriously address the problem of evidence that might be so prejudicial as to distract the jurors from their task. The rules did, however, demonstrate the growing judicial awareness of evidence problems and opened the way for the creation of a full set of adversarial rules of evidence in the eighteenth and nineteenth centuries.

Although the legal mechanism developed between the thirteenth and seventeenth centuries provided the foundation upon which adversarial process was built, judicial activity during this period was not truly adversarial. In 1565, Sir Thomas Smith in his book *De Republica Anglorum* provided a description of the typical criminal felony trial of his day.[8] According to Smith the trial began with the defendant's being brought before the court and asked how he pleaded. Almost invariably the defendant entered a formal plea that he be tried by jury. (The penalty for refusing to plead was severe and persuaded all but the most obdurate defendants to choose the jury.) Local citizens were then called one at a time and seated as members of the jury unless the defendant objected to their participation in the case. After twelve jurors had been seated they were sworn and the hearing commenced.

Usually, the case was prosecuted by a justice of the peace who began his presentation by reading from a written account of his interrogations of the accused and of various witnesses. Next, the victim and other witnesses were produced and questioned. The questioning was initiated by the judge, and as it proceeded, questions were put to the defendant as well as to the witnesses. The questioning most frequently led to a freewheeling discussion, or in Smith's word "altercation," among the witnesses, defendant, and judge. When the judge was satisfied that he had heard enough he called an end to the "altercation," summarized the case for the jury, and charged them to decide it. Frequently, the jury was asked to hear evidence in two or three cases before retiring to deliberate. Once the jury had retired, its members were not allowed to eat or drink until a decision had been rendered.

In Smith's day the judge was clearly an active inquirer (perhaps even prosecutor) rather than a neutral arbiter. The defendant was not represented by counsel and, indeed, was specifically prohibited from having legal representation. The defendant was not allowed to call witnesses, conduct any real cross-examination, or develop an affirmative case. All sorts of evidence could be used in the proceedings, including potentially misleading and prejudicial material like the out-of-court statements read by the justice of the peace. Although the jury was ostensibly neutral and passive, its deliberations were strongly influenced by the judge's remarks and instructions. The judge was free to urge a verdict upon the jury, and, until 1670, jurors who refused to follow the judge's directions could be jailed or fined. Finally, there was no appellate procedure by which the litigants could secure review of the decision. While the germ of the adversarial process may be seen in such proceedings—because they were orally contentious, decided upon the evidence of witnesses, and judged by an arguably neutral and passive jury—they cannot be classified as truly adversarial.

The courtroom routine was more adversarial in the sixteenth and seventeenth centuries in civil litigation than it was in criminal litigation. Even in civil cases, however, the emphasis was not upon adversarial presentation of evidence. Rather, lawyers of that age devoted most of their energy to the fabrication and presentation of pleadings designed to reduce the case to a single, certain, and material question of fact. In order to arrive at this tightly constricted jury question, counsel were compelled by the rules of procedure to refine ever more narrowly their claims by means of a series of writs, motions, and court rulings. At first this winnowing process was conducted before the courts at oral hearings, but in the latter part of the fifteenth century the pleading process came to be based primarily upon written materials. The legal papers involved were measured by the most exacting technical standards and were treated as the most important facet of the case.

The development of legal principles, not the discovery of evidence upon which to resolve disputes between litigants, was of central concern to the bench and bar during this era. The system was not truly adversarial because it dramatically shifted focus away from factual disputes to be resolved by examination of evidence presented in open court. The system was designed to satisfy an astonishing array of formal rules rather than to address the substance of the parties' claims. It confined the proof-presenting process to the narrowest corner of judicial activity. In addition, as in the case of criminal proceedings, the judge played a very active role, there was little protection against misleading or prejudicial evidence, and appellate review was seldom available. With respect to this last point, the only way jury action could be reviewed was by means of a quasi-criminal prosecution of the jurors. This mechanism was woefully inadequate to correct any but the grossest errors or misdeeds. Where appellate review was available it was conceptualized as a challenge to the judge rather than as a continuation of the case or the correction of an error. Further, review was premised on a record that generally did not include the trial proceedings. In sum, there was seldom an effective means by which to appeal adverse factual determinations or breaches of the rules governing trial.

As a final matter it should be noted that between the fifteenth and seventeenth centuries certain judicial mechanisms fundamentally at odds with adversary principles were established. Most important among these was the Star Chamber created in the late 1400s to decide noncapital criminal cases (especially political cases) and to punish misbehaving jurors. Star Chamber practice was based upon the judicial examination of witnesses in camera. Cases were frequently commenced with secret judicial examination of the defendant under oath. Thereafter, other witnesses would be called and privately examined. At the end of the questioning, records of the examinations were used as the basis for the court's decision. One can see in the procedures of the Star Chamber the spirit of an era that had not yet adopted adversary principles. The legislation dismantling the Star Chamber in the 1640s, while motivated by the politics of the time, may be taken as the announcement of a change in English sensibilities and a turning toward adversarial principles.

The Establishment of the Adversary System

Political turmoil engulfed England in the second half of the seventeenth century and triggered dramatic changes. From the 1640s onward the full range of adversarial mechanisms began to grow, and by the end of the 1700s the adversary system had become firmly established not only in England but in America as well. During this period both judge and jury came to conform fairly closely to the ideals of neutrality and passivity. The jury was placed firmly on the road to neutrality in *Bushell's Case* in 1670. Although that case left jurors free to use their own knowledge of a case, the notion of active jury inquiry was on the wane well before 1670. By 1700, decisions rendered at nisi prius (civil cases tried by circuit-riding representatives of the central English courts) could be reversed and a new trial ordered if the judge believed the evidence was insufficient to warrant the verdict. The availability of a new trial in these circumstances bespeaks judicial confidence that the great bulk of the evidence was being heard in open court rather than in private. The new trial mechanism was effectively extended to all cases by Lord Mansfield after 1756. Juror activism was also curbed in other ways during the eighteenth century. Particularly important, after 1705 jurors in civil cases no longer had to be selected from the exact neighborhood in which the case arose. This substantially reduced the likelihood that jurors would have any private information to utilize in making their decisions.

By the eighteenth century the jury came to be seen not only as neutral and passive toward the factual issues in the case but also as a fundamental check on governmental and judicial despotism. Cases like the famous New York trial of Peter Zenger on charges of seditious libel in 1734 and *Bushell's Case* illustrate this trend. In both cases jurors at some personal risk resisted government efforts to use the judicial mechanism to punish political opponents. It is not surprising that when the Constitution of the United States was fashioned in the 1780s there was widespread insistence that it specifically incorporate the right to jury trial as a check on the other institutions of government.

Judicial neutrality and passivity took a longer time to develop. In England the struggle between the principles of royal prerogative and impartial adjudication raged throughout the seventeenth century. The reign of the Stuart kings was marked by repeated royal attempts to manipulate the judiciary and by the frequent removal of judges for political reasons. (The most famous incident of this sort was the removal of Chief Justice Coke by King James I in 1616.) It was not until 1701, when Parliament passed the Act of Settlement, that judges were assured tenure during good behavior. About that time, Lord Holt became chief justice of the King's Bench and significantly altered judicial attitudes toward criminal defendants. Under Holt the courts began to recognize an obligation to protect defendants and to ensure fair trials. The rise of judicial independence and evenhandedness in criminal cases together set the courts firmly on the road to judicial neutrality.

In the United States the struggle for judicial neutrality occurred primarily in the early 1800s. Until then judges might be expected to be political partisans who openly advertised their attitudes in court. After Jefferson was elected, his supporters attempted to remove a number of incompetent or partisan Federalist judges from office by impeachment and conviction. In 1804 John Pickering was removed in this manner, and, shortly thereafter, Supreme Court Justice Samuel Chase was impeached. After a turbulent trial, Chase was acquitted by a single vote in the Senate. Chase's prosecution served as a powerful warning against strident political activity by judges. The neutral posture adopted by Supreme Court Chief Justice John Marshall came to be accepted as the standard by which to measure the propriety of judicial behavior. After 1800 tighter controls were also imposed on the courtroom activity of American judges. Judicial conduct was controlled by applying strict rules of evidence and by placing exacting limits on the remarks that could be made at the close of the case. All of this moved American judges toward neutrality and passivity.

While judges and juries were evolving into neutral and passive fact finders, attorneys were expanding their responsibilities as purveyors of evidence and managers of litigation. The rules of procedure and evidence that facilitated this expansion will be discussed later in this chapter. In addition to procedural changes, the strength and importance of the legal profession increased significantly throughout the eighteenth century. In England, counsel came to have a decisive part to play in both criminal and civil processes. Defendants accused of treason were allowed attorneys in 1695, and throughout the 1700s lawyers were given widening responsibility in felony cases. By 1837 felony defendants were allowed attorneys for all purposes in British courts.

The English bar was highly skilled and well established even before the eighteenth century. Its position was simply enhanced during the 1700s. In the United States the bar was not as well established, but its growth in the 1700s was impressive. Professor Lawrence Friedman, in his book *A History of American Law*, suggests that in 1700 there were few attorneys in America, but that by 1750 there was a competent and successful bar in virtually every major American community.[9] This pattern of growth continued throughout the succeeding two centuries, particularly after 1850. As the number and authority of attorneys increased, so apparently did the vigor of their advocacy. By the first half of the nineteenth century flamboyant courtroom advocacy was the main avenue to success. Lawyers rose to prominence because of their forensic skills, and this aspect of the attorney's work took on paramount importance.

Changes in procedure introduced in the eighteenth and nineteenth centuries shifted legal focus away from elaborate pleadings and debates about fine points of law toward resolution of disputes on the merits. Lord Mansfield was one of those responsible for reform. He worked to reduce use of the rules of procedure as a device for avoiding adjudication on the merits. He fashioned simpler rules where possible and elsewhere sought to persuade litigants to consent voluntarily to the use of streamlined practices. The reforms begun by Mansfield were carried forward by both English and American legislatures. Throughout the nineteenth century the legislatures acted to reduce the technicality and complexity of the legal process. Among the outstanding achievements of this legislative effort were the Field Code adopted by New York in 1848 and the Judicature Acts adopted by the English Parliament in 1851 and 1873. These reforms allowed advocates to devote their energies to the resolution of disputes by the presentation of evidence in open court.

With the growth in importance of the courtroom presentation came heightened sensitivity to evidentiary problems. The law of evidence developed in two directions in the 1700s and 1800s. First, rules were shaped that increased the availability of evidence. Proscriptions incapacitating various witnesses were overthrown. Parties to litigation had, for several centuries, been barred from testifying. After repeated attacks by Jeremy Bentham and others, the rule of party incapacity was abandoned. (The English law on this question was revised in 1851.) Even earlier, Mansfield took the lead in overturning other witness disqualifications including those concerning non-Christians, Quakers (who refused to take an oath), and nonparty witnesses who were in some way interested in the outcome of the litigation. Judicial authority to compel testimony was enhanced during the period. In 1804 English common law courts were given the power, by writ of *habeas corpus ad testificandum*, to require the appearance of any witness. Beginning in 1806 witnesses could no longer refuse to answer questions on the ground that response might lead to civil liability. The effect of all these changes was to open the courts to the testimony of virtually every witness and to increase the burden on the trier of fact to sift and to analyze conflicting testimony.

The second development in the law of evidence in the 1700s and 1800s was the expansion of rules designed to safeguard the neutrality and passivity of the fact finder. Included were regulations intended to insulate the decision maker from misleading or prejudicial material and others designed to prevent the trial judge from taking too active a part in the prosecution of the case. Fundamental to the effort to ensure the integrity of the evidence was an emphasis on cross-examination. Attorneys were encouraged to test virtually every piece of evidence by rigorous cross-examination. Where evidence could not be tested in this way, as in the case of out-of-court affidavits, rules were established to bar use of the evidence in most circumstances. Exclusionary rules were fashioned not only to ensure cross-examination but also to prevent the use of questionable materials. The opinion and hearsay rules were refined as a means of achieving this objective. Where the newly expanded rules of evidence were violated, reversal and retrial could be expected. This sort of enforcement of the rules coupled with limitations on judicial questioning and comment helped to curtail judicial activism. The rules of evidence developed during this period provided a framework within which a truly adversarial contest could be conducted.

The regulation of the practice of law had begun long before the eighteenth century. In the 1200s, rules governing the conduct of advocates were already common. An adversarial code, however, emphasizing zealous representation of each client and loyalty to his cause was the product of the 1700s and 1800s. As proceedings became more adversarial, conflicting ethical demands were exerted upon lawyers. (This was especially likely as attorneys became more frequently involved in criminal cases.) On the one hand, attorneys were expected to be officers of the court and to seek the truth. On the other, they were expected to be keen advocates on behalf of their clients.

These conflicting duties were highlighted in a series of hotly contested trials in the late eighteenth and early nineteenth centuries. One of the most famous involved the prosecution of Queen Caroline on a charge of adultery in 1821. During the course of the proceedings the queen's attorney, Lord Brougham, declared that regardless of personal and political risk he had but a single duty, to represent his client zealously. While this doctrine of single-minded zeal was never officially adopted, it became a fundamental tenet of the adversary lawyer's code. Serving as a counterbalance to this principle was a series of rules curtailing underhanded practices, forbidding tactics designed to harass or to intimidate an opponent, and barring behavior intended to mislead or to prejudice the fact finder. In America, Judge George Sharswood, in a series of lectures given in 1854 at the University of Pennsylvania, delineated a set of ethical precepts placing primary emphasis on zeal and loyalty. These precepts were the model upon which the American canons of professional conduct were based.

The final component of the adversary system to take shape during the eighteenth and nineteenth centuries was appellate review. Until the 1700s there was little review of trial proceedings. Thereafter, the new trial and bill of exceptions grew to maturity and provided a sound basis for review. Coupled with this expansion of appeals was the development in the nineteenth century of courts that did nothing but decide appellate cases. These courts were committed to a careful search of the record to determine if there were error warranting reversal. The emphasis on the search for error may have been what led nineteenth century courts to a preoccupation with technical nicety.

Although the precise reasons for appellate technicality in the nineteenth century are not known, the development of adversarial principles may have had much to do with it. As appellate courts began to see themselves as guardians of a system with precise rules concerning evidence, procedure, passivity, and neutrality, they may have concluded that strict enforcement by means of reversal was the only way to ensure compliance with the new principles. Old habits may have died hard in the lower courts, causing the appellate judges to be even more vigorous in their review. Whatever the cause of strict review, it did help to establish the adversarial principle that trial activity would have to conform to the rules vesting the litigants with control of the process and securing the neutrality and passivity of the fact finder.

Although it is not clear why the adversary process came into its own during the eighteenth and nineteenth centuries, there are a variety of social and economic considerations that may have influenced developments. The 1700s and 1800s were a time of intense social and economic ferment. They were the centuries of the American and French revolutions and of dramatic industrialization. The traditional bases of wealth and power in English society, real property and aristocratic position, were steadily undermined by growing profits from trade and manufacture. Those who profited in the new industries swelled the ranks of the middle class. As this class grew in size and strength, its champions (including Jeremy Bentham, Lord Brougham, and Adam Smith) argued that fundamental changes should be made in the organization of society. Among the changes sought was a significant extension of the franchise. The democratization of the electorate during this era accelerated the shift of power from the landed gentry to urban, energetic, nonaristocratic groups.

The same forces that sought voting rights also pressed for expansion of individual political and economic freedoms. Freedom of speech, of assembly, and of petition were all vigorously asserted and given ever wider recognition. On the economic scene, freedom was associated with the dissolution of social restraints on wages, prices, and profits and with the principle of freedom of contract, allowing each man the right to enter into whatever agreements he thought proper. Economic competition and social change rather than stability became the hallmarks of society. Disappearance of the old restraints released forces that transformed society. Those who could function effectively in the marketplace, like the entrepreneurs and the business corporations, grew in prominence while individual laborers faced greater privation and suffering than they had ever known.

The demise of stability led to a new legal situation. The numbers and sorts of disputes that were brought to the courts grew significantly. Amidst all the conflict and change it is likely that a desire arose for a legal mechanism that could meet the problems of the day and yet preserve some continuity with the more stable past. The adversary mechanism met these requirements. It was an outgrowth of procedures that had been used for several hundred years in England and America. The idea of a neutral and passive fact finder was not a radical departure but rather the extension of trusted and traditional methods. At the same time, the adversary courts were receptive to new claims. They allowed the parties to define the issues and the evidence. They thereby provided a forum for questions that no other institution in society would hear or resolve.

The special needs of eighteenth and nineteenth century society accentuated the adversarial aspects of Anglo-American judicial procedure. Because there were more participants in the legal process and because they were affiliated with different social and economic classes, a demonstrably neutral mechanism was needed. The best means to demonstrate neutrality was by using a disinterested and passive fact finder. The jury readily filled this need. Respect for the principle of neutrality made the courts a credible mechanism for resolving disputes. It also tended to make the courts an open forum to which each new social group could come seeking vindication of its rights. This tradition of openness to new claims of right has continued into the twentieth century.

The element of party control of proceedings apparent in English procedure from the earliest times was also attractive to the intensely individualistic polity of the eighteenth and nineteenth centuries. The English and American judicial process made increasing allowances for each party to run his lawsuit as he saw fit, to voice his claims and to select his evidence. The judicial decision was directly tied to the presentations of the parties. It is not surprising that these facets of procedure were accentuated in an age preoccupied with the establishment of individual political and economic rights.

These tendencies toward adversarial procedure were further

sharpened by the judges and lawyers who controlled the legal system. Members of the bench and bar in both England and the United States were practical men with broad experience. They knew their society and shared the social and economic values it was coming to adopt. Doubtless, in their legal activity they attempted to respond to the needs they perceived. Further, adversarial process was in the interest of lawyers as a group. It created ever more work for attorneys, as increasing numbers of potential litigants sought legal advice, and provided a dramatic public outlet for their forensic skills. Adversary procedure was the right procedure for the times. It did not pose a threat of radical change, but could credibly accommodate the demands of the forces of change at work in English and American society.

Notes

1. Theodore Plucknett, *A Concise History of the Common Law*, 5th ed. (Boston: Little, Brown, 1956), p. 115.

2. Ibid., pp. 109–10.

3. Sir William Holdsworth, *A History of English Law*, 7th ed., 17 vols. (London: Methuen & Co., 1956), vol. 1, pp. 321–32; Plucknett, *A Concise History*, p. 107.

4. *Bushell's Case* was a *habeas corpus* proceeding brought to free a juror who was imprisoned for refusing to pay a fine imposed by the trial judge when he and his fellow jurors would not convict William Penn and William Mead of trespass, contempt, and unlawful assembly.

5. Sir John Fortesque, *In Praise of the Laws of England*, S. B. Chrimes, ed. and trans. (Westport, Conn.: Hyperion Press, 1979), chaps. 25, 26.

6. Plucknett, *A Concise History*, p. 134.

7. John Langbein, *Prosecuting Crime in the Renaissance* (Cambridge: Harvard University Press, 1974), p. 22.

8. Sir Thomas Smith, *De Republica Anglorum*, L. Alston, ed. (1906; reprinted ed., New York: Barnes & Noble, 1972), book 2, chap. 23.

9. Lawrence Friedman, *A History of American Law* (New York: Simon & Schuster, 1973), pp. 81–84.

3
Nonadversarial Elements in the American Judicial System

While it may be confidently asserted that the courts of the United States utilize adversary procedure, there are a number of situations in which the judiciary has either refused to implement adversary principles fully or has allowed deviation from those principles. The most significant area in which adversary procedure has never been completely implemented is in the prosecution of criminal defendants. A brief review of the history of publicly instituted criminal proceedings may help to explain why the adversary process has not been fully extended into the realm of criminal prosecutions.

The Criminal Process

In medieval England formal criminal trials generally followed the pattern described in chapter 2 and were initiated by the injured party. An informal summary procedure was also used, apparently whenever a lawbreaker was apprehended in the criminal act or immediately thereafter. Upon capture the offender was brought before the local court or bailiff, a brief hearing was held, and punishment was meted out at once. The use of a summary procedure continued into the fourteenth century and expressed a community consensus that, whenever possible, known criminals should be swiftly punished without recourse to elaborate trial.

In 1166 the Assize of Clarendon established a grand jury procedure to facilitate royal inquiry into criminal activity not complained of privately. With the growth of this mechanism came a need for more elaborate public prosecutions. Originally, these prosecutions were informal affairs, and jurors from the grand jury that issued the indictment sat on the petit jury that considered guilt and innocence. The use of such jurors virtually ensured conviction and suggests that the courts of the era were far more concerned with the protection of public order than with the perfection of procedures to protect defendants.

With the passage of time the criminal process came to be ever more tightly controlled by royal officials. As described by Sir Thomas Smith, the king's officers in the sixteenth century initiated the grand jury proceedings that led to prosecution, selected and managed the jury that considered the case, and, through the agency of the justice of the peace, presented the case for conviction.[1] The king used the courts to vindicate royal authority. The defendant who was the target of judicial proceedings was not permitted a large part in the process. In felony cases he could not employ the services of an attorney. Generally, he could neither call witnesses nor cross-examine witnesses who testified against him. He could not introduce evidence in his behalf. He could not even appeal an adverse decision. The advantages ceded to the Crown appear to have been arranged to assure the king ample authority to suppress crime. The concept of an evenhanded criminal process designed to encourage a defendant to contest the state's accusations before a neutral and passive fact finder was not generally recognized.

The dangers inherent in this sort of criminal process did not go unappreciated. Although the defendant was not afforded the opportunity to function as an adversary, certain protections were developed to hold government power in check. The three protective mechanisms of greatest significance required the prosecutor, first, to satisfy rules of extreme exactitude and formality in preparing written indictments, second, to overcome a presumption that the defendant was innocent, and third, to persuade all twelve jurors that the defendant was guilty.

The requirement of formality prevented the prosecution from exercising arbitrary control over the charges and evidence to be considered at trial. By contrast the defendant was not bound to make any formal written declaration and could use any sort of defense at trial. The presumption of innocence placed the full burden of proof on the state and enabled the defendant to force the state to make its case. (This mechanism is intimately associated with the development of the principle that the state should not be allowed to force a defendant to incriminate himself.) The unanimous jury rule had an effect akin to that of the presumption of innocence. It placed the burden on the government to convince each of the twelve jurors that the defendant was clearly guilty. These three devices and their corollaries did little to assure the defendant an equal part in the contest. Rather, they protected him by placing a heavy burden upon the state.

Not until the eighteenth and nineteenth centuries were changes introduced into the criminal process to allow the defendant to take a more active part in the proceedings. The role of counsel was steadily expanded during this period, but complete representation in felony cases was not allowed in England until 1837. As the 1700s progressed, the defendant's right to participate in the trial of his case was expanded in other ways. Eventually, the defendant or his representative was permitted to cross-examine the prosecution's witnesses and to introduce witnesses on his own behalf. Rules of evidence were adopted that protected defendants from the use of certain sorts of prejudicial materials. (Among the items excluded were most character evidence and some varieties of hearsay.) Appellate review was established, and courts of appeals were granted authority to reverse wrongful convictions.

The process of reform expanded the options available to the criminal defendant. Modern criminal practice still, however, reflects the ancient reluctance to make the criminal defendant a full participant in all phases of the criminal process. For example, the defendant has no right to have his counsel appear before the grand jury or, in most situations, to obtain any information about its proceedings. The grand jury functions as an inquisitorial body entirely beyond the purview of the defendant.

Further, there is no general rule of reciprocal discovery in criminal cases. In civil cases, each adversary is allowed to make full inquiry concerning the nature of his opponent's proof. No such machinery is recognized in criminal cases. The defendant is allowed some information, but he is not permitted access to all the prosecutor's evidence. The government is not obliged to help the defendant make the best possible case.

Finally, certain rules of evidence serve to bar the defendant from making a complete factual presentation. The defendant is free to choose whether to testify or not, and no adverse inferences may be drawn from his silence. If he does testify, however, his prior criminal record may be used to discredit him. The threat that such information will be used frequently discourages the defendant from taking the witness stand. The criminal record rule has the effect of shrinking the range of evidence a criminal defendant may offer. Other evidentiary rules also disadvantage the criminal defendant, including those allowing liberal use of hearsay on the question of identification and those tightly restricting the use of hearsay that exculpates the accused. In all these circumstances the ancient spirit of nonadversarial criminal procedure is reflected in today's practices.

Nonadversarial Reforms

In a number of settings, courts in the United States have abandoned adversarial techniques. This trend did not begin only recently but rather grew out of social and economic forces that have been building for a long time. The individualistic adversarial approach is, to a significant degree, inconsistent with what Max Weber has described as the fundamental requirements of modern "bureaucratic" government and industry, that official business be dispatched with "utmost speed, precision, definiteness and continuity."[2] Adversarial process, as will later be discussed, is slower and more individualized than some other procedures. These characteristics, among others, have made adversary procedure a target of reformers both inside and outside the judiciary.

Historically, reformers have sought to alter the adversary system in two ways. First, the kinds of cases courts will hear have been limited. In the latter half of the nineteenth century the courts were inundated with suits involving job-related worker injuries and did not prove very adept at handling such claims. Their procedures were slow and their solutions unsatisfactory. Often, injured workers received absolutely no compensation. Legislation took most such claims out of the courts and assigned them to workmen's compensation boards to decide. These boards relied on streamlined administrative methods rather than on full-blown adversary proceedings. In recent times, similar action has been taken with respect to labor disputes, automobile accidents, and medical malpractice claims. Influential commentators, including a number of prominent judges and attorneys, have urged a further narrowing of jurisdiction by the exclusion of cases involving prisoner's rights, antitrust, and civil rights questions.

The number of cases heard has been limited not only by the narrowing of jurisdiction, but also by increasing the pressure for settlement rather than adjudication on the merits. It should be noted that settlement is not necessarily antithetical to the adversary process. In fact, a high percentage of settlements has long been a trait of adversary systems of justice. Today well over 90 percent of all criminal and civil cases are settled, and the percentage of settlements seems to be growing. The Supreme Court has specifically endorsed the movement toward more settlements in criminal cases. In a series of cases decided in the early 1970s, the Court sanctioned plea bargaining agreements (transactions in which the defendant pleads guilty in order to secure a reduced sentence or some other benefit). Although the propriety of such agreements has been hotly debated, the Supreme Court viewed them as essential in dealing with the high volume of criminal work.

The trend toward settlement has created some concern among commentators. Professors Zeisel, Kalven, and Buchholz have argued that there is a "core of cases" that should be tried either because of the nature of the issues involved or because a certain number of trials is needed to ensure the continuing credibility of any adjudicatory system.[3] If the number of litigated cases shrinks too drastically, the continuing efficacy of the system may be called into question.

The second sort of reform employed to deal with demands for "speed, precision, definiteness and continuity" has been to reduce judicial reliance on adversary principles in conducting the business of the courts. Basic components of the adversary system including judicial passivity, advocate responsibility for the development of the case, jury primacy, traditional rules of procedure and evidence, and thoroughgoing appellate review have all been modified. Judicial passivity has been undermined in a number of ways. In the name of efficiency, judges have been admonished to take charge of settlement negotiations at the earliest moment, to supervise the bargaining process, to render opinions concerning issues not yet litigated (as a means of persuading counsel to settle), and to settle as many lawsuits as possible. A large number of judges have adopted these and similar practices without focusing significant attention on the apparent conflict between this approach to settlement and the principle of passivity, which holds that judges should limit their involvement in the compromise of cases lest they become embroiled in the merits and committed to a specified outcome notwithstanding the quality of the proof.

Judicial passivity has come under attack not only in the settlement context but also with respect to the management of litigation. The judge who passively awaits the development of the evidence by the parties is said to be incapable of properly protecting the proceedings from delay and distortion caused by unskilled or excessively contentious counsel. He is also said to be ill-equipped to meet the challenge of complex litigation. To redress these perceived weaknesses the managerial powers of the trial judge have been radically expanded. In recent years, judges have been freed to take an active part in both the preparation and presentation of lawsuits. Judges regularly use tools such as the pretrial conference and pretrial order to determine not only the pace but the content and direction of litigation. Rules regulating judicial involvement in the trial have been steadily liberalized. Judges have been ceded extensive authority to question witnesses called by the parties as well as to call witnesses of their own. The practice of judicial summary of and comment upon the evidence has increased. These changes have appreciably altered the adversary process by encouraging judicial management at the expense of party control of proceedings.

As judicial power has increased, the primacy of the jury in adversary proceedings has decreased. The right to trial by jury has not, in itself, been altered because Article III as well as the Sixth and Seventh amendments to the United States Constitution guarantee the right to jury trial in a wide variety of circumstances. Procedures regulating the way in which jury trials are run, however, have been substantially modified. For centuries it was agreed that the jury was to comprise twelve members and was to render a unanimous verdict. It was also understood that jurors would be impaneled only after opposing counsel had examined each juror under oath (voir dire). All of these procedures have been substantially altered.

In two famous cases, *Williams* v. *Florida* (1970)[4] and *Colgrove* v. *Battin* (1973),[5] the Supreme Court rejected the rule that the jury is required to have twelve members. In each case the Court approved the use of as few as six jurors. (In *Ballew* v. *Georgia* (1978),[6] the Court drew the line at six, holding that five-person juries were of insufficient size to perform the adjudicatory function.) In two more important cases, *Johnson* v. *Louisiana* (1972)[7] and *Apodaca* v. *Oregon* (1972),[8] the Supreme Court held that a unanimous verdict was not required in state court criminal trials. In arriving at these conclusions the Supreme Court did not consider the effect of change on the jury as a neutral and passive decision maker. In fact, empirical analysis has demonstrated that changes regarding jury size and unanimity have reduced the neutrality of juries. Research indicates that smaller juries are less likely to engage in reliable deliberations and are less likely to consider minority points of view.[9] These changes have reduced the attractiveness of the jury to litigants and have effectively narrowed its utility in the adjudicatory process.

In a series of decisions in the middle 1970s, the Supreme Court significantly curtailed the right of counsel to question prospective jurors. In *Ristaino* v. *Ross* (1976),[10] the Court held that voir dire questioning was almost entirely within the discretion of the trial judge and could be sharply limited in most cases. In *Ross* the Court approved, in effect, the impaneling of potentially biased jurors except where the facts of the case "were likely to *intensify* any prejudice individual members of the jury might harbor."[11] *Ross* expanded tolerance of juror prejudice and reduced the likelihood of neutrality. Again, change struck at the heart of the adversary value of the right to jury trial.

The procedural and evidentiary rules governing the adversarial process have also been the target of reformers. A wide range of reforms have been adopted that sacrifice adversarial principles. Perhaps most significant is the large number of rules that enhance the discretionary powers of the trial judge. Professor Maurice Rosenberg of the Columbia Law School has estimated that in as many as forty procedural situations the Federal Rules of Civil Procedure have been construed to allow for the exercise of judicial discretion.[12] This sort of expansion of judicial discretion undermines the judge's passivity and reduces the ability of the advocates to direct the proceedings. Judicial discretion has also been expanded in the Federal Rules of Evidence. Material previously banned as prejudicial may now be admitted at the court's discretion. Further, changes in the evidence rules cede the trial judge increased power to control fundamental processes like cross-examination, determination of preliminary questions of fact, and the use of hearsay evidence.

Finally, the likelihood of thoroughgoing appellate review has been subject to significant limitation. Although an absolute right to review has never been established, it is generally agreed that, at least in criminal cases, the defendant will be allowed a minimum of one appeal. The Supreme Court helped to ensure this result by guaranteeing indigent criminal defendants appointed counsel to press their first appeal, by requiring that indigents be provided transcripts if a written record is necessary for appeal and by requiring the waiver of fees that would otherwise bar the impecunious from filing a criminal appeal. These decisions are now so firmly rooted that it seems unlikely appellate review in criminal matters will be directly curtailed. By contrast, the Court has limited appellate review in the last few years by endorsing rules that

- limit access to appeal in civil cases (by upholding the requirement of a filing fee with respect to civil appeals)
- reduce the scope of appeal in all cases (by approving the ever expanding application of the doctrine of "harmless error," which states that no judgment shall be reversed unless the error or defect *substantially* affects the rights of a party)
- diminish the availability of review beyond the first appeal (by holding that criminal defendants have no right to the appointment of counsel beyond the first appeal)

In summary, although the predominant means of resolving disputes in American courts is the adversary system, a variety of nonadversarial mechanisms have been incorporated into the judicial process. Some of these are of ancient lineage, especially in criminal cases. In recent years, however, a steadily increasing number of nonadversarial techniques have been adopted in all sorts of cases.

Notes

1. Sir Thomas Smith, *De Republica Anglorum*, L. Alston, ed. (1906; reprinted ed., New York: Barnes & Noble, 1972), book 2, chap. 23.

2. Max Weber, *Max Weber on Law in Economy and Society*, Max Rheinstein and Edward Shils, ed. and trans. (Cambridge: Harvard University Press, 1954), p. 350.

3. Hans Zeisel, Harry Kalven, Jr., and Bernard Buchholz, *Delay in the Court* (Boston: Little, Brown, 1959), p. 108.

4. 399 U.S. 78.

5. 413 U.S. 139.

6. 435 U.S. 223.

7. 406 U.S. 356.

8. 406 U.S. 404.

9. For a summary of such research see Richard Lempert, "Uncovering 'Nondiscernible' Differences: Empirical Research and the Jury-Size Cases," *Michigan Law Review*, vol. 73, no. 4 (March 1975), p. 644.

10. 424 U.S. 589.

11. 424 U.S. at 597 (emphasis added).

12. Maurice Rosenberg, "Appellate Review of Trial Court Discretion," *Federal Rules Decisions*, vol. 79 (September 1978), p. 173.

4
Criticisms of the Adversary System Considered

Critics have, in recent years, vigorously attacked the adversary system, claiming that it is flawed. These attacks have profoundly affected the debate concerning retention of adversary procedure and have greatly facilitated the adoption of nonadversarial methods. The two most frequently voiced criticisms are that the adversary process is too slow to serve the needs of modern society adequately and that it sets too low a value on the discovery of material truth.

The Pace of Adjudication

It must be admitted at the outset that adversary procedure relies on mechanisms that appreciably slow adjudication. Adversary theory requires the judge to remain passive until the conclusion of the advocates' presentations. He is not free to conduct an independent inquiry or otherwise accelerate the pace of the proceedings. The judge's passivity undoubtedly slows adjudication. When a jury is used as decision maker, proceedings are even slower because of the extra time spent selecting the jurors and presenting the case.

Although the requirement of passivity slows the judicial process, important considerations justify this result. The decision maker's passivity is relied upon in the adversary system to ensure that the trier will remain neutral until he renders his decision. Neutrality, in turn, tends to ensure the integrity of adversary deliberations. In this context, as well as a number of others, the adversary system may sacrifice speed to protect the probity of the process.

The rules of procedure that regulate the adversary contest also slow the pace of litigation. Adversary procedure assures each party ample opportunity to prepare and to present his case. This preparation and presentation time, dependent as it is on the vagaries of legal practice and advocate efficiency, does not lead to nearly as swift a decision as would a process primarily concerned with judicial inquiry rather than party presentation. By allowing both sides to be heard in full, however, the adversary process tends to expand the pool of information available to the fact finder. This arguably increases the likelihood the trier will be able to render a decision that satisfies the needs of the litigants.

The use of a strict set of rules of evidence to prevent the introduction of prejudicial or misleading information also slows the adversary process. Before evidence may be introduced, its source and trustworthiness must be stipulated or demonstrated. Testimony from witnesses may be elicited only through a series of precisely formulated questions. These procedures invite careful scrutiny of each question and each answer. This careful control of the fact-gathering process undoubtedly slows the tempo of adversary proceedings. Again, the adversary approach rejects celerity to improve the quality of deliberations.

Finally, the adversary process relies upon appellate review to ensure obedience to the codes regulating litigation. In effect, the appellate mechanism gives each party a chance to be heard at least twice. Appellate review undercuts the finality of judgment and thereby allows litigants to prolong the adjudicatory process substantially. Here, as in the previous examples, the adversary method may sacrifice speed to enhance the integrity of deliberations.

Almost every procedure in the adversary process moves at a measured pace rather than at maximum speed. Delay, or perhaps more accurately, deliberation, has been built into every aspect of the adversary system. If one adopts the view that any diminution in speed is a serious danger, then every part of the adversary process is open to challenge. The problem with this sort of challenge is that it fails to focus on the most important question, whether there is a need for a process that is careful, deliberative, and committed to airing the claims of each litigant fully rather than one that proceeds at maximum speed. As will be argued in the following chapter, there is a real need for a legal mechanism controlled by the litigants and devoted to the resolution of their claims. A deliberate pace is valuable because it encourages the careful scrutiny of each claim and increases party involvement in and control of the judicial process.

Moreover, there is little evidence that adversary procedures cause more delay than nonadversary alternatives. A recent study conducted by Thomas Church, Jr., for the National Center for State Courts, found that courts exercising the greatest effort to avoid adversarial trials by inducing settlements were also the courts in which litigants were most likely to experience long delays in getting their cases resolved.[1] Similarly, Professor Hans Zeisel and his associates, in their classic study of court delay, found that the use of adversarial juries actually speeded cases to final resolution in many circumstances.[2] Analyses like these suggest that adversary mechanisms may not be a fundamental cause of unnecessary delay in adjudication.

The Discovery of Material Truth

The second frequently voiced criticism of the adversary system is that it sets too low a value on the discovery of material truth. At the heart of this criticism is the notion that various parts of the adversary mechanism inhibit the development of a historically accurate picture of what happened on the relevant occasion and that this is likely to deter the fact finder from reaching a just decision. The three facets of the adversary system most strongly condemned as inhibitors of the discovery of truth are party control of the information-gathering process, zealous and single-minded representation of each litigant by his attorney, and evidentiary rules that circumscribe the types of information available to the decision maker.

Before reviewing these specific criticisms, three general points should be considered. First, although chapter 1 of this study suggests that the adversary process places somewhat more emphasis on the resolution of disputes than on the discovery of material truth, it need not be conceded that the process is inept at finding truth. The adversary process is open to an extremely broad range of information. Indeed, adversary courts probably hear more detailed and divergent testimony than courts using judge-centered methods of inquiry. Justice Benjamin Kaplan of the Massachusetts Supreme Judicial Court, formerly a professor at Harvard Law School, compared the fact-gathering efforts of American and West German courts.[3] He concluded that America's party-controlled courts receive significantly more information than West Germany's judge-directed courts, because the adversary courts hear at least two distinct versions of the facts in every case. Further, these versions are likely to be the product of intensive pretrial investigation. (Pretrial inquiry is quite limited in Germany and in other civil law countries.) Considering the information-gathering potential of the parties, it is debatable whether the adversary approach is any less effective at uncovering truth than is a judge-centered alternative.

Second, one must keep human limitations in mind when defining judicial objectives. The weakness of human perception, memory, and expression will often render the discovery of material truth impossible. To become preoccupied with truth may be both naive and futile. It is to the advantage of the adversary system that it does not define its objectives in such an absolute and unrealistic fashion.

Third, a preoccupation with material truth may be not only futile but dangerous to society as well. If the objective of the judicial process were the disclosure of facts, then any technique that increases the prospect of gathering facts would be permissible. Spouses could be compelled to testify against one another, psychoactive drugs could be used to loosen the tongues of reluctant witnesses, and even torture could be employed in certain situations. Between 1300 and 1800 the inquisitorial judges of Europe functioned within a system of criminal procedure that placed special emphasis on the discovery of truth. The outcome of this approach was wholesale reliance on torture. Today no Western judicial system accepts such methods. Truth is not the end the courts seek. Truth is nothing more than a means of achieving the end, justice. The disclosure of material facts is not the only means of achieving justice, and to treat it as the end is to open the way to unsavory abuses.

Party Control of Litigation. Critics of the adversary system argue that parties should not be allowed to control the information-gathering process because they cannot be trusted to present all the relevant evidence. Rather, the parties are likely to provide only the information that they think helps their cause. This sort of presentation is said to skew the proof in ways that undermine the accuracy of the final determination. Litigant control is also criticized because it allows each party to confer freely with all the witnesses and to assist witnesses in preparing their testimony. This investigation and preparation procedure is said to pose two sorts of threats: first, the subtle transmutation of testimony by means of psychological suggestion; second, the subornation of perjury.

In response it should be remarked that party control is necessary to preserve the neutrality of the fact finder. If the judge is assigned the task of making factual inquiry, both theoretical analysis and empirical data suggest that his biases are likely to be intensified and his decisions opened to prejudicial influence. This loss of neutrality is arguably as significant a problem as any skewing caused by party control.

Litigant direction yields benefits besides neutrality. Psychological experiments have indicated that when parties in an adversary system find themselves at a factual disadvantage, they will expend significant effort to improve their position. This tends to bring the proof presented at trial into balance and to ensure a decision based upon more complete information than would otherwise be the case. Another advantage of party control is that it is likely to reduce "impositional costs" by minimizing the chances that judges will render uneconomical decisions poorly fitted to the needs of the litigants.

While there is solid evidence to support the principle of party control of the witness selection and examination process *at trial*, caution may be warranted with respect to endorsement of rules allowing the adversaries to interrogate freely and to prepare all witnesses *before trial*. Recent psychological studies by Professor Elizabeth Loftus of the University of Washington suggest that the testimony of eyewitnesses and other disinterested informants may be substantially altered by the manner in which they are interrogated before trial.[4] There may be substantial danger in allowing uninhibited pretrial interrogation not only because it will influence the witness's story but because later cross-examination is not likely to demonstrate that new material has been insinuated into the witness's recollections. (Not even the witness is likely to recognize that this has occurred.)

The solution to this problem is far from clear. On the one hand, parties need the freedom to make thorough inquiry in order to prepare their cases. On the other hand, thorough inquiry may cause irremediable taint. The answer lies in limiting pretrial interrogation while allowing parties to gather the information they need. (One solution would be to allow the parties pretrial access to all witnesses but only during formal proceedings of which a record were kept.) Whatever the precise answer may be, this problem is not so serious as to warrant the overthrow of the system.

Zealous Representation of the Litigant. Attorneys have, from the earliest times, been viewed as obstructors of truth. The basis for this view is not hard to identify. Attorneys are skilled advocates. Their facility with words and procedure gives them the means of manipulating the information-gathering process. When the advocate lends his talents to the single-minded pursuit of the goals of his client, it is not hard to understand why onlookers might consider him the enemy of veracity. The ethical rule that compels the attorney zealously to represent his client officially reinforces loyalty at the expense of commitment to the search for truth.

In response it should first be noted that attorney zeal is directly linked to party control of proceedings and that the arguments in favor of party control also support zealous representation of the litigant. This is so because the complexity of legal proceedings makes it virtually impossible for parties to proceed without counsel. It has frequently been suggested that the attorney can serve his client and, at the same time, ensure that the truth is disclosed. This position fails to preserve attorney zeal and loyalty because it requires the attorney to act as an agent of the court whenever there is a potential conflict between his client's interests and the pursuit of material information. The likely results of casting the attorney in this impossible situation are unethical conduct if the lawyer chooses to act on behalf of his client in a doubtful case and substantial discouragement of client candor, cooperation, and trust if the lawyer chooses to act on behalf of the court.

This does not mean that an attorney can never be required to act in ways that oppose his client's wishes. When a client asks his lawyer to aid him in the commission of a crime or in the perpetration of a fraud, the attorney can and must reject such overtures. The situations in which the attorney must reject his client's wishes should be clearly and narrowly defined, however, otherwise a chill will be cast over the relationship and over the entire adversary process.

Strict Evidentiary Code. The rules of evidence prohibit a wide range of information from being presented to the fact finder. No matter how useful or important certain items may be, if they fall afoul of the evidence rules they cannot be considered. This applies to most words spoken out of court (hearsay) as well as to such facts as a party's criminal record or the existence of insurance. In all this the critics see a substantial barrier to the disclosure of important facts and, hence, an impediment to the discovery of truth.

As in the case of attorney zeal, the rules of evidence serve, at least in part, to preserve party control of litigation. They achieve this result by curtailing judicial power over the admission and exclusion of evidence. The rules also directly protect the neutrality of the fact finder. While each rule may not be defensible on this ground, the general thrust of the rules is to insulate the decision maker from unreliable or prejudicial evidence. The protective function is of special importance when lay jurors decide cases. Protection also takes on added importance in the American adversary system because facts are presented only once, at the trial level. In these circumstances insulation from misleading material seems crucial because taint cannot be overcome by a *de novo* hearing on appeal.

Access to the Judicial System

Critics have advanced a number of other objections to the adversary system. They have argued that the American system fails to allow any but the wealthy and powerful access to counsel and the courts. The cost of litigation is said to be so great that the vast majority of Americans cannot afford to participate in the system. Substantial evidence indicates that cost does exclude some from participating in the justice system. Exclusion does not, however, result from any characteristic intrinsic to the adversary method but rather to the means by which it is presently implemented in the United States. Because the problem is not inherent in an adversarial system, it does not warrant the scrapping of the system. What is required is reform of the social and economic conditions that exclude a sizable segment of the population from access to the courts.

Recent American legal history contains a significant number of examples of efforts to expand the availability of legal services. The United States Supreme Court, in a number of precedent-setting decisions, starting with *Gideon* v. *Wainwright* (1963),[5] has required that every criminal defendant who faces the prospect of jail be provided an attorney and the means to prepare his defense adequately. This mandate has measurably increased participation in the process. While it would be unrealistic to claim that *Gideon* has solved all the problems in the criminal setting, it is clear that progress has been made.

Access has been facilitated in civil as well as criminal litigation. The development of the contingency fee as a means of financing litigation has opened the courts in many cases. (In such cases the attorney proceeds without a fee in the hope of sharing in the fruits of victory.) The creation of the Legal Services Corporation appreciably expanded the availability of low-cost legal assistance to the poor. The courts themselves have helped to improve access to judicial remedies by allowing litigants to proceed on behalf of others as well as themselves in cases in which individual claims might not justify the expense of litigation. Class actions and cases involving institutional reform have provided at least a partial remedy to the market failures involved when litigants with serious claims cannot afford to press their grievances. None of these mechanisms has been problem-free, but each has helped to lessen the exclusionary effect of the cost of litigation. Much remains to be done to improve access in civil cases. The American Bar Association and other bar groups appear to be moving in the proper direction with their proposals to increase each lawyer's obligation to undertake *pro bono* work.

The problem of exclusion is not unique to adversarial systems. Professor Inga Markovits of the University of Texas has suggested that the didactic and collectivistic attitudes of East European Socialist judicial systems greatly inhibit citizens from pursuing various individual claims.[6] This observation points out that very different judicial systems can pose practical problems of exclusion for certain classes of claimants. The problem of exclusion may be beyond remedy. What is of importance is a willingness to recognize such problems and to undertake efforts to ameliorate them whenever possible. So long as a society works to improve access to its judicial mechanism, criticism based on exclusion does not justify radical change.

The Power of the Attorney

A number of perceptive critics have argued that the attorneys upon whom the adversary system relies have become too dominant a force in the litigation they prosecute. The value of the adversary system is, in large part, attributable to party involvement in the litigation process. When the attorney comes to play too decisive a role, he can short-circuit the benefits of party control. In such circumstances the parties are likely to feel that they have not had a hand in the adjudication of the case and that they are not bound by the mandates of the court. Attorney domination can also cause an increase in "impositional costs" by focusing the litigation on the lawyer's interests rather than on the client's needs.

At present, it does not appear that the problem of attorney control is so grave as to threaten the integrity of the adversary system. Further, corrective mechanisms within the adversary framework help to ensure that the attorney will serve his client's interests. Perhaps most significant are the ethical rules governing attorney behavior. These compel the attorney to solicit and to obey his client's instructions with respect to settlement and crucial strategic decisions during the course of litigation. While it is uncertain whether attorneys will obey such rules, the heightened awareness of the lawyer's ethical responsibilities created by the Watergate scandal and reinforced by the American Bar Association's continuing activism in the ethics field provide a basis for optimism. In cases of serious deviation from a client's instructions, the injured litigant can seek damages in a malpractice action. The expanding scope of attorney malpractice liability has the beneficial effect of providing a means of enforcing the ethical rules regulating consultation and control.

Conflicting Judicial Responsibilities

A final criticism of the adversary system warranting discussion is that it places the trial judge in the untenable position of having to perform inconsistent or conflicting tasks. Marvin Frankel devotes a chapter of his book *Partisan Justice* to one aspect of this problem.[7] He asserts that because the judge is obliged to control the litigation and the litigants, it is extremely difficult for him to remain neutral and passive. According to Frankel the judge is likely to become the "target" of one or both of the parties as soon as he exercises his authority.

They will attempt to lure the judge into committing reversible error as a means of ensuring victory on appeal if they are not successful in the trial court. As a defense, argues Frankel, the judge becomes "adversarial," and loses the neutrality and passivity upon which the system depends.

The accuracy of Frankel's description of the judicial situation is not beyond challenge. A significant body of literature supports the proposition that judges in the adversary system generally do not view their situation as adversarial and do not allow themselves to be drawn into the contest. The sensitive judicial officer may indeed feel some strain. This is not surprising in a system designed to control tightly the judge's discretion and to place significant power in the hands of the parties. It would appear, however, that judges generally do not allow such personal feelings to override their professional obligation to deal dispassionately with the cases that come before them. To help maintain equilibrium in the courtroom the adversary system relies on the jury rather than on the judge as fact finder. The interposition of this neutral body of laymen tends to reduce the likelihood of clashes between judges and lawyers.

A second aspect of the problem of conflicting judicial responsibilities involves the judge's duties as lawmaker. One of the primary functions of the judge in the adversary system is to fix the legal rules that will be applied in resolving each case. With some frequency, the legal rules to be applied are so vague, unformed, or out of date that the judge must take it upon himself to fashion the law. Critics argue that this sort of active lawmaking is in conflict with the principles of judicial neutrality and passivity. In point of fact, the law-fixing function does not conflict with neutrality or passivity. The history of the adversary system described in chapter 2 of this study suggests that judges took a significant step toward neutrality when they placed the fact-finding function in the hands of the jury and began to devote their energies to the development of legal doctrine.

Despite this historical evidence, one could maintain that there is a difference between *declaring* law for the benefit of the fact finder and *making* law. In the latter context one could argue that the judge becomes an active advocate committed to vindicating his newly coined legal doctrine. The Anglo-American common law system has never relied on an all-inclusive code of legal principles. Instead the law has been developed on a case-by-case basis, establishing only those rules necessary to resolve the litigated issue. This choice, one of ancient and honorable lineage, makes it inevitable that judges will be lawmakers as well as law declarers. While there is some danger that judges may come to see themselves as advocates on behalf of the legal principles they fashion, the system has established certain controls to limit this prospect. Foremost is appellate review. The courts of appeals in the adversary system are the primary lawmakers. Their review checks judicial excesses in the trial courts and fixes legal principles that serve as an authoritative guide to trial judges.

Although several of the most frequently advanced criticisms of the adversary system are not well founded, the system is not without its faults. Upon examination, however, it appears that none of these is so serious as to warrant the abandonment of adversary procedure. The following chapter will demonstrate the special worth of the adversary system and will consider the defects in the judge-dominated system most likely to be offered as an alternative.

Notes

1. Thomas Church, Jr., *Justice Delayed: The Pace of Litigation in Urban Trial Courts* (Williamsburg, Va.: National Center for State Courts, 1978), p. 32.

2. Hans Zeisel, Harry Kalven, Jr., and Bernard Buchholz, *Delay in the Court* (Boston: Little, Brown, 1959), p. 4.

3. Benjamin Kaplan, "Civil Procedure—Reflections on the Comparison of Systems," *Buffalo Law Review*, vol. 9, 1960, p. 409.

4. Elizabeth Loftus, *Eyewitness Testimony* (Cambridge: Harvard University Press, 1979), pp. 88–109.

5. 372 U.S. 335.

6. Inga Markovits, "Law or Order—Constitutionalism and Legality in Eastern Europe," *Stanford Law Review*, vol. 34, no. 3 (February 1982), p. 513.

7. Marvin Frankel, *Partisan Justice* (New York: Hill and Wang, 1980), pp. 39–58.

5
Defense of the Adversary System

A fundamental lesson of Anglo-American legal history is that traditional methods of resolving disputes have served as a rampart against government tyranny. In light of this insight, reform of the judicial machinery should be approached with caution. The historical evidence will not support a flat refusal to change (innovation has been an important element in English and American law since the medieval period), but it does counsel caution where significant departures from previous practices are contemplated. Therefore, even if there were little good to say about the adversary system, those who argue for change would still face a significant burden of persuasion.

Benefits of Party Control of Litigation

A number of reasons, apart from the historical, warrant reliance on adversarial methods. The adversary process provides litigants with the means to control their lawsuits. The parties are preeminent in choosing the forum, designating the proofs, and running the process. The courts, as a general rule, pursue the questions the parties propound. Ultimately, the whole procedure yields results tailored to the litigants' needs and in this way reinforces individual rights. As already noted, this sort of procedure also enhances the economic efficiency of adjudication by sharply reducing impositional costs.

Party control yields other benefits as well. Perhaps most important, it promotes litigant and societal acceptance of decisions rendered by the courts. Adversary theory holds that if a party is intimately involved in the adjudicatory process and feels that he has been given a fair opportunity to present his case, he is likely to accept the results whether favorable or not. Assuming this theory is correct, the adversary process will serve to reduce post-litigation friction and to increase compliance with judicial mandates.

Adversary theory identifies litigant control as important to satisfy not only the parties but society as well. When litigants direct the proceedings, there is little opportunity for the judge to pursue his own agenda or to act on his biases. Because the judge seldom takes the lead in conducting the proceedings, he is unlikely to appear to be partisan or to become embroiled in the contest. His detachment preserves the appearance of fairness as well as fairness itself. In legal proceedings, as the United States Supreme Court stated in *Offut* v. *United States* (1954), "justice must satisfy the appearance of justice."[1] When it fails to do so, social credibility is eroded and distrust introduced.

There is little direct evidence of the extent of personal or societal acceptance of adversarial processes as contrasted with other types of adjudicatory processes. A number of multinational surveys, however, including those conducted by Professors John Thibaut and Laurens Walker, have found that a majority of subjects will designate adversary procedure as the fairest for resolving disputes.[2] This finding lends support to the argument that adversary procedures are perceived as fairest and are more likely to satisfy litigants and onlookers than nonadversary alternatives.

Thibaut and Walker have provided significant empirical evidence that litigant control produces other sorts of benefits.[3] First, it tends to encourage desirable conduct on the part of litigants and their counsel. Psychological experimentation has shown that an advocate working in an adversarial context who finds his client at a factual disadvantage will expend significant effort to improve his client's position. This is to be contrasted with the behavior of the advocate working in an inquisitorial setting who will seldom undertake an extensive search for better evidence to bolster a weak case. The adversary process appears to encourage advocates to protect parties facing an initial disadvantage and hence to improve the overall quality of the evidence upon which adjudication will be based.

Thibaut and Walker have also found that adversarial emphasis on party presentation tends to counteract the bias of the decision maker more effectively than does an approach requiring the active participation of the trier in marshaling the proof.[4] This finding provides tangible support for the theoretical assertion that the best decision maker is one whose *sole function* is adjudication. Because the adversary process assigns the prosecutorial function to the parties, it serves to increase the likelihood that the trier will be able to devote his full attention to a neutral adjudication of the case.

The adversary process assigns each participant a single function. The judge is to serve as neutral and passive arbiter. Counsel is to act as a zealous advocate. According to adversary theory, when each actor performs only a single function the dispute before the court will be resolved in the fairest and most efficient way. The strength of such a division of labor is that individual responsibilities are clear. The possibility that a participant in the system will face conflicting responsibilities is minimized. Each knows what is expected of him and can work conscientiously to achieve a specifically defined goal. When participants in the judicial process are confronted with conflicting obligations, it becomes difficult for them to discharge any of their duties satisfactorily. The more frequently they face conflict, the more likely it is that they will not perform their assigned part or will not perform it in a way that minimizes conflict rather than fully discharges their responsibilities. Among the greatest dangers in this regard are that the judge will abandon neutrality if encouraged to search for material truth and that the attorney will compromise his client's interests if compelled to serve as an officer of the court rather than as an advocate. In either case the probity of the process is seriously undermined.

Party control has another beneficial effect as well. It affirms human individuality. It mandates respect for the opinions of each party rather than those of his attorney, of the court, or of society at large. It provides the litigant a neutral forum in which to air his views and promises that those views will be heard and considered. The individualizing effect of adversary procedure has important implications besides those involving individual satisfaction. The receptiveness of adversary procedure to individual claims implies that adversary courts will take a sympathetic view of the claims of individuals against the state. The prospects for sympathetic hearing are increased because the judge and, to an even greater extent, the jury are beyond governmental control and cannot be taken to task for their decisions.

These propositions concerning the receptiveness of adversarial courts to the claims of individual citizens are, at least in part, borne out by historical evidence. For centuries adversarial courts have served as a counterbalance to official tyranny and have worked to broaden the scope of individual rights. The steady expansion of doctrines to protect minorities both in England and in the United States reflects this fact. When adversarial process has been ignored in the operation of the courts, as in the days of the Star Chamber, human rights diminished and governmental repression increased.

We live in an era of expanding government power. The urgency of social problems, including the scarcity of resources and the exigencies of national defense, tends to lead the government to exert pressure on the citizenry to cooperate in ensuring the efficient operation of society as a whole. This pressure poses a keen threat to the maintenance of individual rights. In these circumstances, there is a need to preserve the kind of institution that will sympathetically review claims based on individual rights rather than on governmental necessity or the common good. Because the adversarial courts are primarily committed to hearing and to upholding the claims of individuals, they are most likely to be capable of handling this task.

Constitutional Recognition of Adversarial Procedures

Any defense of the American adversary system would be incomplete if it did not consider the constitutional status of adversarial procedure. The adversary process has not, as a whole, been made the immutable law of the land by incorporation in the Constitution. Significant parts of the adversarial mechanism, however, are recognized in the Constitution or have been held by the Supreme Court to be constitutionally required. The text of the Constitution does not specify what form of judicial procedure shall be used in the courts of the United States. It does, however, incorporate a great deal of adversarial machinery. Article III of the Constitution specifies that judges "shall hold their Offices during good Behaviour, and shall at stated Times, receive for their Services a Compensation, which shall not be diminished during their Continuance in Office." This provision does not protect an exclusively adversarial mechanism, but it does help to ensure an independent judiciary, a key element in any adversarial system. Article III also specifies that the trial of crimes shall be by jury. Again, the text does not require adversary procedure, but helps to encourage it, at least in criminal cases, by mandating the use of the most neutral and passive of fact finders.

The most important constitutional recognition of adversary procedure is to be found in the Sixth and Seventh amendments to the Constitution. The Sixth Amendment requires that a jury be available in all criminal cases and that the accused have the right "to be confronted with the witnesses against him, to have compulsory process for obtaining witnesses in his favor, and to have the Assistance of Counsel for his defence." Taken together these requirements go a long way toward establishing adversary procedure in criminal cases.

The Supreme Court has held that implicit in the confrontation requirement is a strong predisposition in favor of the cross-examination of witnesses in open court and a preference for live testimony in general. The compulsory-process clause adds to these requirements the principle that the defendant has the right to present a defense. These rights together seem to call for an adversarial process in which each litigant is given an opportunity to present his case. The right to counsel takes this idea one step further. It has been construed to require the state to make counsel available to all defendants, thereby increasing their effectiveness as litigants. The mandate for counsel has other implications as well. When considered together with the other requirements of the Sixth Amendment, it has been held to bar states from controlling the order in which the accused presents his proof at trial and to guarantee that the defendant be granted an opportunity to make closing argument.

The Seventh Amendment, which addresses civil litigation, does not specify nearly so much as does the Sixth. It does, however, preserve the right to jury trial in civil cases and specifies that "no fact tried by jury, shall be otherwise re-examined in any court of the United States, than according to the rules of the common law." This latter requirement seems to envision a process of adjudication and review of the sort utilized in adversarial proceedings.

In addition to these specific prescriptions, the Fifth and Fourteenth amendments state that no person shall be deprived "of life, liberty, or property, without due process of law." These words have been viewed as requiring a fair trial in a fair forum in both civil and criminal cases. To what extent this mandate compels adversary procedure is open to question. In criminal cases, the Supreme Court has viewed the due-process requirement as fixing the principle of judicial neutrality. Even the appearance of partiality has been condemned. Further, the due-process clauses have been held, in association with the requirements of the Sixth Amendment, to protect a defendant's right to make a full defense. Although no right of appeal has been discovered, either in the due-process clauses or elsewhere, the Fifth and Fourteenth amendments have been construed to require states that do provide a criminal appeals process to open it to the poor as well as to the rich. This requirement has gone a long way toward establishing a criminal appellate system.

Civil litigation has been less affected by the due-process clauses than has criminal litigation. Beyond the basic mandate of fairness just what process is "due" has never been specified. At a minimum, judicial neutrality, some opportunity to present evidence, and the right, at one's own expense, to be represented by counsel seem to be protected.

The determination that the Constitution requires an array of adversarial mechanisms, especially in criminal proceedings, suggests that our courts and perhaps the framers of the Constitution have viewed adversary process (or at least its essential components) as fundamental to a fair judicial system. Constitutional endorsement of the adversary system makes change particularly inappropriate.

Comparison of Adversarial and Inquisitorial Processes

To compare adversary procedure with its most likely replacement will help in assessing the value of the adversary system. Without doubt, the most likely substitute for adversary procedure is some variant of the judge-centered inquisitorial process used in most European countries. The first step toward understanding such a procedure is to identify its attributes. The key actor in the inquisitorial process is the judge. It is his duty to investigate the facts and interrogate the witnesses as well as to formulate the decision. The entire adjudicatory process revolves around the judge. Because he is so important, lay juries are not favored. For the same reason party control of the proceedings is minimized. Generally, the parties initiate the proceedings and participate in the inquiry, but they are never allowed to control the fact-gathering process. Lawyers play a far less important role than they do in the adversary system. As one might expect, the inquisitorial process is firmly committed to the search for material truth.

Since the objective of the inquisitorial process is likely to be material truth, few technical rules of evidence or procedure are recognized. The judge is relatively free to conduct the inquiry as he sees fit. He can ask for virtually any sort of information (except for items protected because of extrajudicial concerns like those expressed in the marital or priest-penitent privileges). Proceedings are run in the most informal fashion, more like the American pretrial conference than an evidentiary hearing. The proceedings are not recorded in a verbatim transcript. Rather, the judge extracts what he thinks is important and records it. On appeal, all issues in the case, both legal and factual, are open to review, and new evidence can be submitted on all points. This is in marked contrast to Anglo-American procedure, which narrowly circumscribes review of factual determinations and seldom allows the introduction of new evidence on appeal. Finally, the inquisitorial process relies on a rather large judicial bureaucracy arranged in a hierarchal structure. Judicial responsibilities at each level of the system are specified in detail, and strict conformity is required. Innovation or variation is generally not tolerated.

An inquisitorial approach to adjudication is open to several criticisms. First, the inquiring judge is more likely to act upon his biases than is his adversarial counterpart. The late Professor Lon Fuller of Harvard Law School described what generally occurs:

> At some early point a familiar pattern will seem to emerge from the evidence; an accustomed label is waiting for the case and, without waiting further proofs, this label is promptly assigned to it. It is a mistake to suppose that this premature cataloguing must necessarily result from impatience, prejudice or mental sloth. Often it proceeds from a very understandable desire to bring the hearing into some order and coherence, for without some tentative theory of

the case there is no standard of relevance by which testimony may be measured. But what starts as a preliminary diagnosis designed to direct the inquiry tends, quickly and imperceptibly, to become a fixed conclusion, as all that confirms the diagnosis makes a strong imprint on the mind, while all that runs counter to it is received with diverted attention.[5]

Second, the inquisitorial approach is less sensitive to claims concerning individual rights. It is committed to material truth. This commitment was so strong between 1300 and 1800 that judicial officers felt warranted in using torture to pursue the facts in the criminal litigation before them. Modern inquisitorial process has clearly rejected such methods, but the emphasis on material truth remains. This emphasis relegates questions of individual rights to a subsidiary position in the litigation.

Generally, the inquisitorial process will not serve as a check on government power. Inquisitorial judges (at least throughout Europe) are bureaucrats who identify with the government and whose advancement in the judicial hierarchy depends on accommodation rather than confrontation. Such officials are not likely to identify novel rights against the government or expand rights previously established. Further, inquisitorial judges are not likely to be inclined toward the creative use of judicial authority in any context. Advancement in the bureaucracy is not won by creative activity but rather by conformity to the rules of the organization. The successful inquisitorial judge is the one who conforms his conduct to the previously established organizational boundaries.

The European inquisitorial systems have, in recent years, expanded their use of adversarial techniques in some settings. (From the nineteenth century on, continental court systems have been borrowing procedures from the Anglo-American model.) Professor Michele Taruffo of the University of Pavia has noted this trend in the behavior of counsel. According to Taruffo, despite the commitment of the inquisitorial process to the search for material truth, attorneys in the various West European systems have come to view themselves as zealous advocates whose goal is the vindication of their clients' interests.[6] Professor Markovits has even discovered a turning toward adversarial ways in the Socialist legal systems. The Socialist courts have begun to recognize claims involving the rights of individuals and to permit counselors to press such claims. The adoption of adversary procedure does not seem imminent in Europe, but the adversary model has been treated as offering a variety of advantages that are attractive alternatives to inquisitorial methods.

The proud history and constitutional status of the adversary system as well as the benefits to be derived from its individualizing effect are strong reasons for its retention. Adversary procedure has served as a guardian of individual liberty since its inception. It has facilitated the extension of personal rights to a wide range of minority groups. Given these facts and the absence of a clearly superior alternative, the American commitment to the adversary system ought to be maintained.

Notes

1. 348 U.S. 11, 14.

2. John Thibaut and Laurens Walker, *Procedural Justice, A Psychological Analysis* (Hillsdale, N.J.: Lawrence Erlbaum Associates, 1975), pp. 77–80, 94–96.

3. Ibid., pp. 38–39.

4. Ibid., pp. 49–51.

5. Lon L. Fuller, "The Adversary System," in Harold Berman, ed., *Talks on American Law* (New York: Random House, 1961), pp. 38–39 (quoting from the *Report of the Joint Conference on Professional Responsibility of the American Bar Association*, 1958).

6. Michele Taruffo, "The Lawyer's Role and the Models of Civil Process" (paper presented at the International Conference on Ethics and Responsibilities of the Legal Profession, Tel Aviv, Israel, August 17–21, 1980).

6
Using Nonadversarial Means to Resolve Disputes

The adversary method is not equally useful in resolving all types of disputes. The suggestions in the preceding chapter identify several situations in which the adversary process would seem particularly useful. The most important of these is litigation involving a dispute between a citizen and the government. In such a dispute, whether it be a civil rights case, a criminal matter, or a contract action, the adversary judge and jury serve as a vital counterbalance to the power of the state.

Nonetheless, there are settings in which adversary procedure does not seem appropriate. When the parties must continue to work or to live together in intimate contact or in a cooperative relationship, the adversary method may not be the best means of resolving their dispute. Adversary procedure may exacerbate rather than resolve tensions and may not foster the kind of compromise essential to the restoration of harmony. For this reason, disputes between labor and management or between family members in an intact family unit, for example, should usually be resolved in nonadversarial proceedings.

It is also sensible to utilize nonadversarial methods when all the parties strongly desire speed, simplicity, and economy in adjudication. In such settings the adversary process will tend to intrude undesired deliberation and expense. The labor grievance process is an example of a case in which certain adversary procedures are avoided for reasons of economy and celerity. Finally, where there is no dispute, adversary machinery is not needed. In an uncontested divorce, an adoption, or a change of name, there is little call for the panoply of procedures built into the adversary process.

Although it is possible to list types of cases that seem suited to adversarial adjudication, any a priori designation threatens to exclude some litigants from access to procedures they view as essential to the proper consideration of their cases. An arbitrary ban on adversarial consideration of repetitious cases, or cases involving small sums of money, or cases involving institutional relationships raises serious problems of social and political judgment as well as accusations of unequal treatment. A better approach than categorical exclusion may be a system that allows the parties to choose the type of process best suited to their needs. Where all the parties make an *uncoerced* choice to avoid the adversarial process, it seems eminently sensible to honor their decision. Use of an election mechanism may ease the burden on the adversarial courts, while protecting the rights of those who believe they cannot obtain redress outside the adversarial framework.

Only when the nature of the adversary process and the values it vindicates are clearly understood and considered is it possible to determine the extent to which nonadversary processes should be utilized by American courts to resolve disputes. If these issues are ignored, intelligent change is impossible.

Selected Bibliography

Cappelletti, Mauro, and Jolowicz, John Anthony. *Public Interest Parties and the Active Role of the Judge in Civil Litigation.* Dobbs Ferry, N.Y.: Oceana Publications, 1975.

Clinton, Robert. "The Right to Present a Defense: An Emergent Constitutional Guarantee in Criminal Trials." *Indiana Law Review* 9: 713–858

Conlon, Timothy. "The Role of Public Interest Litigation." *Law and Social Problems* 1: 115–44.

Damaska, Mirjan. "Evidentiary Barriers to Conviction and Two Models of Criminal Procedure: A Comparative Study." *University of Pennsylvania Law Review* 121: 506–89.

———. "Structures of Authority and Comparative Criminal Procedure." *Yale Law Journal* 84: 480–544.

Frank, Jerome. *Courts on Trial: Myths and Reality in American Justice.* Princeton, N.J.: Princeton University Press, 1949.

Kaplan, Benjamin, von Mehren, Arthur T., and Schaefer, Rudolf. "Phases of German Civil Procedure I." *Harvard Law Review* 71: 1193–1268.

Landsman, Stephan. "The Decline of the Adversary System: How the Rhetoric of Swift and Certain Justice Has Affected Adjudication in American Courts." *Buffalo Law Review* 29: 487–530.

Langbein, John. "The Criminal Trial before Lawyers." *University of Chicago Law Review* 45: 263–316.

———. *Torture and the Law of Proof.* Chicago: University of Chicago Press, 1977.

Lea, Michael, and Walker, Laurens. "Efficient Procedure." *North Carolina Law Review* 57: 361–78.

Nelson, William. *Americanization of the Common Law: The Impact of Legal Change on Massachusetts Society, 1760–1830.* Cambridge: Harvard University Press, 1975.

Ploscowe, Morris. "The Development of Present-Day Criminal Procedures in Europe and America." *Harvard Law Review* 48: 433–73.

Saltzburg, Stephen. "The Unnecessarily Expanding Role of the Trial Judge." *Virginia Law Review* 64: 1–81.

Schlesinger, Rudolf. "Comparative Criminal Procedure." *Buffalo Law Review* 26: 371–85.

Thayer, James Bradley. *A Preliminary Treatise on Evidence at Common Law.* South Hackensack, N.J.: Rotham Reprints, 1969.

Weston, Peter. "Confrontation and Compulsory Process: A Unified Theory of Evidence for Criminal Cases." *Harvard Law Review* 91: 567–628.

———. "Order of Proof." *California Law Review* 66: 935–85.

Selected AEI Publications

Uniform Rules of Criminal Procedure for All Courts, Russell Chapin with W. Graham Hueber (66 pp., $4.95)

Equal Opportunity: On the Policy and Politics of Compensatory Minority Preferences, Allan P. Sindler (27 pp., $2.95)

Meeting Human Needs: Toward a New Public Philosophy, Jack A. Meyer, ed. (469 pp., cloth $34.95, paper $13.95)

The Federal Antitrust Laws, Fourth Revised Edition, Jerrold G. Van Cise (92 pp., $4.95)

Private Enforcement of the Antitrust Laws: An Economic Critique, Warren F. Schwartz (33 pp., $3.25)

Regulating International Business through Codes of Conduct, Raymond J. Waldmann (139 pp., cloth $12.25, paper $5.25)

Significant Decisions of the Supreme Court, Bruce E. Fein.

1978–1979 Term (199 pp., $6.25)

• *Mail orders for publications to:* AMERICAN ENTERPRISE INSTITUTE, 1150 Seventeenth Street, N.W., Washington, D.C. 20036 • *For postage and handling, add 10 percent of total; minimum charge $2, maximum $10* • *For information on orders, or to expedite service, call toll free 800-424-2873* • *When ordering by International Standard Book Number, please use the AEI prefix—0-8447* • *Prices subject to change without notice* • *Payable in U.S. currency only*

AEI Associates Program

˞erican Enterprise Institute invites your participation in the competition
rough its AEI Associates Program. This program has two objectives:
˒ public familiarity with contemporary issues; and (2) to increase
˓ issues and disseminate the results to policy makers, the academic
˒lists, and others who help shape public attitudes. The areas
˒ Economic Policy, Education Policy, Energy Policy, Fiscal
˒ulation, Health Policy, International Programs, Legal
˒udies, Political and Social Processes, and Religion,
˒. For the $39 annual fee, Associates receive
ˡ*um*, the newsletter on all AEI activities
˒d all supplements
ˑooks
ˑinars on key issues
ˑications: *Public Opinion*, a bimonth-
ˑs of public opinion on social and
ˑhly journal examining all as-
AEI Economist, a monthly
ˑluating future trends (or

fo˞

Call 202/8˞   ˡSE INSTITUTE
  11˓   ˑ D.C. 20036